Copyright © 2003 by Christine West

All rights reserved. No part of this publication may be reproduced, stored in a retrieval system or transmitted in any form or by any means, electronic, mechanical, photocopying, recording or otherwise, without written permission from the publisher. For information contact info@keynotebooks.com

Cover design by Connie West
Book Design by KeyNote Books
Author photograph by Paul Wiese
Website design by Craig Bettridge
Logo design by Chromasia Design and Paul Wiese

Editorial Advisors:
Helen Polaski - Compiler of Forget Me Knots…from the Front Porch
Vanessa K Mullins - Senior Editor/Compiler of Nudges from God
Maureen Allen - Writer for Bellaonline.com
Jozette Aaron - aka Georgie DeSilva (If I Would Love Again, Next Stop)

Printed in the United States of America
First printing 2003

ISBN 1-58961-058-X

 **KeyNote Books®**

Attention: Additional Copies

To order additional copies of *Service With A Smile* ☺ *Waiter / Waitress Training*, please contact the following:
For speedy delivery and ultimate savings go to:
www.keynotebooks.com
or send inquiries to orders@keynotebooks.com

Or refer orders to:
www.thegreatamericanbookstore.com
www.bn.com
www.amazon.com
www.borders.com
Ingram Distribution
Baker & Taylor
Books in Print

Customized editions can be designed to meet specific needs i.e., addition of company logos and personalized introductions. Discounts available for quantity orders. For more information write to info@keynotebooks.com

Dedication

Special thanks to my best friend, who suggested, encouraged and believed in all that this book entails, from its concept and contents to its author.

Cheers to you, Mom!

Service With A SMILE

Waiter / Waitress Training

by Christine West

Includes **1001** Tips

For Making

BIGGER TIPS

Acknowledgements

Thank you to all of the interviewed servers and diners, without whom this training guide would not have been possible.

For your time, interest and invaluable input, I extend my gratitude. The excellence of this guidebook is accredited to you as much as it is to me.

TABLE OF CONTENTS

FOREWORD	1
INTRODUCTION	4

PART ONE

GETTING A FOOT IN THE DOOR AND PUTTING THE RIGHT FOOT FORWARD   8

Chapter 1: Resumes and Interviews	10
Chapter 2: Looking the Part	20
Chapter 3: Always be Prepared	26
Chapter 4: Service with a Smile ☺	32
Chapter 5: Know Your Stuff	34

PART TWO

LEARNING THE TRADE   48

Chapter 6: Take notes	50
Chapter 7: Teamwork - Do Unto Others	52
Chapter 8: Economizing Steps + Maximum Efficiency = Maximum Tips	56
Chapter 9: Making the Boss Sit up and Take Notice	62
Chapter 10: Sell! Sell! Sell!	66
Chapter 11: Wining and Dining	84
Wine Glossary	88

PART THREE

FINE TUNING — 108
Chapter 12: Above and Beyond - Dazzling the Customer — 110
Chapter 13: Table Maintenance — 116
Chapter 14: Prioritize and Organize — 120
Chapter 15: Scan and Plan — 124
Chapter 16: Read Your Tables — 126

PART FOUR

THE HEAT IS ON — 130
Chapter 17: Dealing With Complaints — 132
Chapter 18: Don'ts — 136
Chapter 19: Safe Serving — 138
Chapter 20: S#*~ Happens — 142
Chapter 21: Responsible Alcohol Service — 146

PART FIVE

CHECK, PLEASE — 152
Chapter 22: Turn 'em and Burn 'em — 154
Chapter 23: Check, Please — 156
Chapter 24: Finishing the Job — 160
Chapter 25: Bartenders, Bar Servers, Cocktail Servers, Drink Slingers, etc. — 162

Chapter 26: Tips   164

Glossary   **170**

PART SIX

APPENDIXES   **174**

Appendix A   175
    Top Ten Customer Pet Peeves Regarding Servers

Appendix B   176
    Top Ten Server Pet Peeves Regarding Other Servers

Appendix C   177
    Popular Red Wines Often Found in Restaurants and the Foods Which They Best Accompany

Appendix D   179
    Popular White Wines Often Found in Restaurants and the Foods Which They Best Accompany

Appendix E   181
    What About Hot, Spicy Food and Wine?

Appendix F   182
    Why Drink Rosé

Seminars With A Smile ☺   184
Suggestion Box   185

FOREWORD

As the final stage of research, the author enlisted a panel of servers with varying levels of experience to review *Service With A Smile* ☺. The following are unedited testimonials by servers from all over the world:

This book has made me appear to be the fastest learner in the industry. My boss and trainer are both astounded with how fast I've caught on to serving. They think I'm a whiz kid. But it's time to confess: I owe my knowledge and extraordinary tips to Service With A Smile ☺. *Thank you, Christine.*

- ***Barbie from Australia - 3 months experience***

Living in the largest city in the world opens one up to many job opportunities; also it makes for a very competitive industry. I now have the confidence and know-how to compete with the best. This book has enabled me to move up to a busier restaurant.

- ***Sherise from Mexico City – 1 year of experience***

Tourists are the most experienced diners of all, and Service With A Smile ☺ *helped me to give service above and beyond my customers expectations. I have received more compliments since I read this book than I have in my entire time as a server.*

It's easy for customers to stiff a server when they know they'll never see them again, but not so easy if the service is impeccable.

- ***Jennifer from New Orleans - 5 years of experience***

Reading this manual has been a humbling experience for an arrogant veteran like me. Merely flipping through the pages, I found new ways to dazzle my customers and co-workers, even more than usual. The combination of writing skills, research and serving experience certainly shine through. Trust me when I say, Service With A Smile ☺ *is very impressive!*

- **Gerald from Los Angeles - 26 years of experience**

Having watched my father run his own restaurant since I was a baby, I thought that serving would be no problem. Boy, was I in for a surprise! This book came along at the perfect time. After reading Service With A Smile ☺ *I'm making tips like I never imagined, and I've reorganized the dining room to be more efficient. My fellow servers are actually showing signs of respect to the boss's daughter. Even a stubborn man like my father is impressed. He wants to know how he can order more copies for the rest of his staff? Thank you!*

- **Angelica from Puerto Rico - 5 months experience**

I had no idea how much I didn't know about wine, etiquette, style and how to improve my tips. Tips! Tips! Tips! Who says waitpersons don't have a pension plan? With a great city at my feet and this book in my hands, I may just open a little place of my own and train my staff with Service With A Smile ☺.

- **Pat from Las Vegas - 9 years of experience**

This book has improved my knowledge and tips so much, I no longer have to rely on my parents for tuition and books. When I'm a famous fashion designer, I'll insist that the caterers for my galas have trained their staff with Service With A Smile ☺.

- **Sheila from Paris - 3 years experience**

My confidence level is at an all-time high thanks to your fantastic manual. No more mumbling and faking it when I'm not sure how to handle situations.

Also, my mom spotted the book on my desk and couldn't resist snooping. She's pleased to say that it has helped her to be a fabulous hostess at dinner and cocktail parties and to show off for her snooty wine club.

- ***Anthony from Toronto - 2 years of experience***

When I put some of the theories and strategies into practice, I was truly impressed with the way my tips skyrocketed. I've never read such an informative training guide. As a server trainer, I've convinced my boss to implement this book as the foundation of our resort's training program. We're ordering 50 copies to start.

- ***Lorenzo from Jamaica - 17 years of experience***

I was extremely skeptical. Given my many years as a waitperson, I opened the book prepared to criticize all that it had to offer. Some areas seemed a bit obvious to a veteran like myself, but there was so much I was able to take away from the book, that I appreciate the obvious as the great reminders that they are. The reminders were only outweighed by the knowledge that even I was able to learn a few new tricks of the trade.

- ***Leslie from London - 32 years of experience***

A server on a cruise ship, people expect nothing but the best from me. Until I read this book, I thought I was giving them exactly that. I take it with me on the ship to show it to servers everywhere. This is a gift to our profession and needs to be shared.

- ***Jackie from the U.S. to the far reaches of The Caribbean 14 years of experience***

INTRODUCTION

Whether you're a career server, who's in the service industry for the long haul, or you're just waiting tables to supplement your income while you're in school, this book is for you. Whether you're looking to learn the basics of serving or interested in honing your existing skills, this book is for you.

Service With A Smile ☺ is not merely a book. It is the premier reference book on serving. When you've finished reading, you'll gladly place it at eye level on your bookshelf for easy access.

Before you read on, ask yourself the following questions.

- **Do you want to make tips?**
- **Do you want to make more tips?**
- **Do you want to do less work to make more tips?**
- **Do you want to get bigger sections and the best shifts so that you can make more tips?**
- **Do you want to work confidently and efficiently making tips in an establishment that suits you?**

If you've answered yes to any or all of these questions, then you owe it to yourself and your wallet to keep reading.

As a server, you don't have a fixed wage; your potential

income is limitless, provided you have the know-how and motivation to get out there and earn those tips. Don't misunderstand, no one is promising that this book will have you jet-setting with Donald Trump or Bill Gates, but it can help you maximize your tip potential and make your job much more enjoyable and effortless.

What qualifies any one person to write this book?

Nothing!

It must be emphasized that this book is not solely from my point of view. Nearly five years have been dedicated to interviewing and surveying servers and customers in order to provide you with the facts and a diverse compilation of information.

The 100 servers, whom I've interviewed, work in bars, bistros, cafés, chain restaurants, corporate establishments, diners, ethnic cuisine eateries, fine dining establishments, French service restaurants, honky-tonks, inns, lodges, Mom and Pop places, motel dining rooms, pubs, roadhouses, smorgasbords, taverns, theme restaurants, and truck stops. These 100 servers have experience ranging from 6 months to 32 years, tallying up to over 1000 years of collective experience.

The 1000 randomly surveyed customers come from a wide variety of ages, races, financial positions, and ethnicities. From the frequent and the fussy to the occasional and the undemanding, the surveyed diners all had something to contribute.

So, as you can see, one person did not write this book. And it is certainly not a boring textbook written with you as an afterthought. *Service With A Smile* ☺ is for you, the one in the trenches. It is to you, about you, and for you, the server or wannabe server.

Why Did I Write This Book?

This book was researched, compiled and written for servers, restaurateurs and diners alike, but mostly for servers.

The better we are as servers, the happier the customers are. The happier the customers are, the more they'll tip. Also, it doesn't hurt your job security that your boss will be pleased with you because the customers are happy.

Let me say, again, you don't have to be a professional/career server to benefit from this book. Perhaps you're between jobs. Perhaps you're just biding time until your lottery numbers are announced or waiting for that big inheritance. Whatever your story, you can never make too much money, and there's always room for improvement.

Improvement. That's why this book was written. After searching high and low, I couldn't find a solid book on the realities of serving based on daily applications. There are already more than enough books, training videos, and slogans out there written by pseudo, guru know-it-alls who've never stepped foot in a restaurant or bar except as customers. It's time somebody gave something back to the servers who give so much of themselves every time they strap on an apron.

Not to criticize typical training procedures, but rather than merely being trained by one or even several co-workers, this book gives you the opportunity to receive guidance from 101 of your peers. It gives you the chance to become privy to over 1000 years of collective service experience.

So, I'd like to say, *congratulations!* By purchasing *Service With A Smile* ☺, you have taken matters into your own hands as well as the first step toward maximizing your tips.

FYI → About the language of serving

Some establishments choose to refer to their clientele as guests rather than customers. Reason being, the word 'guest' is supposedly more inviting than the word 'customer.' Without getting into a debate on semantics, this book will call a spade a spade and a customer a customer. I mean, really, when was the last time you asked a guest in your home to pay for dinner and leave a gratuity? Hey, that might not be such a bad idea.

You've heard the terms waiter, waitress, and server. For the purposes of this book, I'll more often lean toward the politically correct 'server'.

While we're on the topic of how to word things, it should be said that we'll be using some common restaurant jargon. You may want to review the glossary at the back of the book before continuing. After having done so, meet me back at part one.

PART ONE

GETTING A FOOT IN THE DOOR AND PUTTING THE RIGHT FOOT FORWARD

In This Part

Chapter 1: Resumes and Interviews

Chapter 2: Looking the Part

Chapter 3: Always be Prepared

Chapter 4: Service with a Smile ☺

Chapter 5: Know Your Stuff

SERVER'S NOTES

Chapter 1

Resumes and Interviews

Dictionaries define a resume as *"a brief account of one's education, experience, previous employment, and interests, usu. submitted with a job application."*

Some less technical ways to view the resume are: a resume is a foot in the door, a sales pitch for which you are the product, a professional way to show off, an acceptable way to tout your own horn. In a nutshell, a resume is an invaluable tool needed for securing a job.

Although many restaurants will want you to fill out an application, you should still have a neat, informative, one-page (two at most) resume available, as well as a typed list of references (personal as well as professional, but no relatives). A comprehensive resume allows an employer to assess your qualifications quickly in the pre-screening process before interviews.

 **FYI →** Did you know that most resumes are initially read for only 15 seconds or less! Your mission is to design a document that will help the readers form mental pictures of you and your abilities.

Technique and Appearance

The first impression of your resume should intrigue the reader to look further. Well organized material, with an easy-to-read size and type of font, correct grammar and spelling and up-to-date information are vital to accomplish this. Resumes should be printed on good quality paper and must be absolutely free of errors.

- Prepare a positive document to present your skills. Now is not the time to be modest. But do not lie! Sell the real you. Any misrepresentation is bound to come back to haunt you, if not in the interview, then on the job.
- There is no one all-encompassing resume. You must create a document that sells your strengths. Market what makes you different from anyone else wanting that job.
- Your enthusiasm, confidence, reliability, and communication skills are revealed through both the content and style of your writing.

Job Objective or Career Goal?

The difference in wording can speak volumes as to your intentions. "Career Goal" tends to refer to a desired position that has a longer term association, while "Job Objective" can refer to an interim or more temporary type of position.

Education

Tell it like it is. You don't need a Masters Degree to be a server.

Work Experience

There are two types of resumes. The chronological style resume is the most widely accepted format for outlining work history. Try the functional model if you have limited related experience.

Chronological Resume

A chronological resume highlights an applicant's previous work experience.

- Organize jobs in reverse chronological order, stating:
    - Start dates and end dates using words, not numbers, i.e., June, not 06
    - Job title (create an accurate one if you had none)
    - Name of company or organization and location
- In point form, talk about what you contributed to or accomplished on the job.
- Personalize your resume: do not use generic points seen in advertisements. Employers complain that it is too difficult to determine the distinguishing qualities of applicants.
- Indicate the level of responsibility you were entrusted with, i.e., depositing cash, managing department during absence of supervisor. Ask yourself if you did more than was required of you by your supervisor. If yes, be sure to indicate the circumstances and outcome.
- Be sure to use the present tense of the verb for continuing work and the past tense for work that has ceased.
- In less relevant work, emphasize transferable skills such as ability to work under pressure, communication skills, attention to detail, etc.).
- Do not use abbreviations, slang, sarcasm or humor; save that for an interview if it feels appropriate.
- Do not use personal pronouns, such as *my*, *their*, or definite and indefinite articles, such as *a*, *an*, *the*.
- Prioritize the points when you are describing your work as they relate to your job objective, not as they related to your previous job.

Functional Resume

A functional format would be an ideal choice for individuals who:

- Have little or no relevant experience, but do have qualifications for the job.
- Have relevant experience but the positions would be lost among the other jobs in a chronological resume.
- Have a number of similar work experiences which would require repeating the same points under several job listings.
- Have so much good material to say that it would take over three pages to do it.

The work experience section is very different from that in the chronological resume as it is divided into two parts entitled "Qualifications" and "Work History".

The Qualifications section should comprise the individual points of the job descriptions as organized by major functions or skills. Identify three to five major areas required for the position being sought (i.e., customer service, teamwork skills, organizational skills).

The Work History section should comprise, in reverse chronological order, a listing of your employment: date, job title, company/organization, location (no job description details). It is important that this, like the rest of the resume, be correct and concise.

It is essential that you have a solid, detailed chronological resume from which to work, as it is difficult to think creatively and evaluate information at the same time.

Other Tips

- Do not include the word, "Resume" at the top of the page or the date you prepared the document.

- Ensure that your name is at the top of all pages.
- Aside from name, address, telephone number(s), no other personal information is required. Age, race, marital status, religion and such things need not be mentioned.
- Use a dictionary and thesaurus to understand and accurately express your skills/abilities for the job.
- Check your first draft for accuracy and thoroughness.
- Check your final copy for errors before printing.
- Do not overuse any one word or vague verbs to describe skills i.e.: *assisted, handled, aided, involved, participated.* Such words do not say precisely what you did.
- Also, on the topic of verbs, avoid weak verbs such as had, did, helped.
- Do not use nouns when talking about your contribution (i.e., organization of new banquet facilities) because what *you* did is not defined precisely enough. Use verbs in a solid sentence, i.e., organized, bartended for large banquet style parties.
- Avoid terms such as *duties included, involved in, worked on, responsible fo*r, *participated in,* because nouns follow these words, and your achievements are not understood.
- If your resume seems to flaunt more about your last job(s) and you want to change direction, no problem. Rather than listing your past jobs in terms of the duties and responsibilities, explain those experiences in a manner that tells why your previous work has gained you the qualities and abilities to fulfill your newly desired position.
- The more in-depth the material and your preparation, the more informative your resume will be to the prospective employer,

and the easier it will be for you to answer subsequent interview questions.
- Preserve all notes from which you prepared your resume on file and add to them periodically (annually/bi-annually) information about your recent activities, job, etc. so that you will always have up-to-date data to generate future resumes.

Before printing a stack of copies, check the final draft of your resume to be sure you haven't missed any of the above details.

For the finer points on resume writing, read a book on the subject, take a course, ask a friend for help.

> Russ, server of 9 years, saved a customer's life one night. A woman was choking, and he administered the Heimlich maneuver, forcing a piece of chicken into flight and saving the woman's life.

Another bit of advice is, if it feels right don't be afraid to mention (on a resume, on an application, or at an interview) special skills, hobbies, activities, or knowledge. For example, CPR or first aid training, a second language, team sports, charity work, unique abilities or skills.

> Laura, server of 4 years, is fluent in sign language. A group from a local hospital for the hearing impaired was so impressed by her, their bus goes to her place of work once a week, insisting on sitting in her section. In fact, when she went to work elsewhere, her dedicated regulars followed her.

Granted, Russ and Laura's stories are precise examples of rare circumstances, but you may possess other talents which could make you a valued commodity for a restaurant.

- Having previously worked at a day-care, as a babysitter, or a volunteer at a kids hospital or library would prove you are good with children. A family restaurant would undoubtedly see that as an asset.
- A history of team sports shows that you work well with others. Many applications or interviewers will ask you about your interest in team sports. When they ask such questions, they're not nearly as concerned about your athleticism as they are about your ability to work as part of a team.
- Do you spend a lot of time with your senior citizen grandparent? Have you ever given your time to other seniors? If so, a restaurant that caters to older clientele will appreciate you.

This brings other concerns to mind. You've taken the time to sell yourself to a boss. Now don't neglect to realize that you're worth the time it takes to place yourself in an establishment that suits you. Think about who you are, your likes and dislikes, your disposition, your personal taste, your strengths and weaknesses.

What am I saying? Work is work, right? Well yeah, but there's more to it than that. Sometimes we have to take what we can get because we have bills to pay. A brutal fact of life. Still, before settling everyone owes it to himself or herself to do anything possible to find a job in an establishment that best suits the individual. Before saturating the market with form resumes, consider submitting them in batches, spread out over a couple weeks or a month. Make an A-list of the places you'd most like to work, a B-list of beauty-queen-runner-ups (so to speak) and a C-list of last resorts.

Before you submit batch A of your preferred options, consider the following:

- If you're a night owl, who reaches peak form when the sun goes down, will slinging bacon and eggs at 6 a.m. really be the job for you?
- If you're outspoken and animated by nature, is a hoity-toity, closed-mouthed atmosphere somewhere you want to spend twenty to forty hours per week?
- Hf you're a vegetarian, who cringes at the sight of red meat, are you going to be able to pull off the role of a steakhouse server?

When you've found an establishment that suits you, and they've taken an interest in you, the next step is the interview.

There are no big secrets regarding an interview. Just be sensible, punctual, confident and prepared. Have an extra copy of your resume on hand in case they've misplaced the original or you need to refer to dates. If your resume says "references available upon request" be sure to have a neatly typed list of your references, their phone numbers, and your relationship to them. Bring a pen and some paper (who knows). Bring copies (keep originals) of any letters of recommendation from previous employers, even if the work wasn't in a related field.

Most importantly, be yourself. Putting on airs may get you a job, but when the real you inevitably comes out, will the boss still think you're suitable for the position? Try to relax, but don't be too relaxed, unemployment is not to be taken lightly.

A helpful hint regarding cover letters is to address the letters to the service manager of each establishment by name (or the person in charge of hiring service staff). How are you supposed to know who that is? Simply call the restaurant and ask.

> Steve, service manager of 12 years, told me about the time an applicant looked him straight in the eye and said, "This is just something I plan to do until I get a 'real job'."
>
> Well, Steve cut the interview short, thanked the young woman for her application, and explained briefly that he had to get back to work. He didn't add that it was 'real work' he was getting back to, yet he's sure the applicant got the picture as she slithered out with her tail between her legs.
>
> I'm going to tell you now, what Steve didn't waste his time telling the applicant then. There's nothing more real than paying your bills. There's nothing more real than a hard day's work. There's nothing more real than the instant gratification you get from a great tip for a job well done. Then there are the times when you give a table all you've got, and they stiff you. It doesn't get any more real than that.

It's a well-prepared applicant who knows a little about the place to which they are applying.

- Call the establishment and make some anonymous inquiries.

- Or better still, pop in before the interview and have a meal, a drink, or a coffee. While you're there, ask your server a few questions. Find out how long they've been in operation. Is it privately owned, or does it belong to a corporation? Does the server who's waiting on you like working there? And if you have a comfortable report with the server, ask what the tips are like.

- Check the menu for selection, prices, etc.

- Pay attention to décor, atmosphere, lighting, style, special boards, etc.

- Look around while you're there for postings or plaques on walls or write ups in menus which tell the history or status of the establishment.
- Surf the internet to see if the establishment has a website.
- Check local newspapers for previous articles.

If a perspective employer asks you, "Why do you want to work for us?" NOW what would you say to show your interest in and knowledge of the organization based on your research?

FYI → Be sure never to call or visit during busy times. The time to apply or inquire is at business lulls, not during rush hours. 94% of the interviewed servers go job hunting between two and four o'clock in the afternoon.

Lastly, we all know there's never a second chance to make a great first impression. Most old-school and many new-school dining establishments' uniforms are black pants/skirts and white shirts/blouses.

After a great deal of research as to why black and white are traditional server colors, the answers to this query were many and conflicting. The consensus was, whatever the reason(s), you can make a great impression by wearing black and white to an interview. If you look like a duck and you quack like a duck...

Chapter 2

Looking the Part

You, the server, have more contact with customers than all other restaurant employees combined, making it your duty to perform at your best and to look your best. Fellow servers and customers alike agree that servers should maintain impeccable hygiene and wear only tasteful accessories. The words "hygiene" and "tasteful" encompass several topics. Let's start at the top of your head and work our way down to the tip of your toes.

Hair

For those with short hair, it's a no-brainer. Clean and neatly styled are the criteria for your hair.

Long hair should always be worn up or pulled back off the face. The big-haired-bimbo-server-of-the-80s-look is passé. Nobody wants to find hair in their food. If they do have a hair woven through their pasta, you're the first person they'll point a finger at. And who can blame them? Do the math:

hair in food + server with unkempt hair = server's fault.

You don't have to cut your hair to cut yourself out of the equation. Even if it's not a house rule, look professional by wearing your hair tied back.

Makeup

Keep it real.

Names like Tammy Fay Baker and Mimi Beaubeck from The Drew Carey Show come to mind. Remember that you're a server, not one of the main attractions at the circus.

Facial Hair

Faces should be kept clean shaven. Men with beards are advised to keep them properly trimmed.

Perfume, Cologne and Deodorants

Wearing underarm deodorant or antiperspirant is recommended, where excessive amounts of perfume or cologne are unacceptable. Aside from the obvious fact that people in restaurants are trying to eat and will probably find that your fragrance conflicts with the aromas of the food, many are allergic to various scents. Going without or using minimal is advisable.

Clothes/Uniform

A clean, pressed, appropriately sized uniform should go without saying, but one disheveled fad that must be addressed is the loosely tucked shirt. If your uniform is to be worn tucked in, please do so neatly and thoroughly.

Maintaining a uniform without rips or buttons missing, and with finished hems is imperative.

Pants or skirts should be a comfortable, tailored-looking fit and not be faded or worn out. Polyester may not be a fashion statement, but it's less likely to fade. And nylons or tights must be free of runs, holes, or snags.

 **FYI** ♀ Tip for female servers. Fed up with sagging pantyhose? Rather than tugging and hiking them up every ten minutes, wear a second pair of panties over (yes over) your pantyhose.

Aprons and Towels

Aprons should be clean and neatly tied or clasped. If you keep a towel on your person for carrying hot plates or wiping your hands on, be sure it isn't tattered or soiled. Change it throughout your shift if necessary.

Jewelry

Less is more. Aside from the fact that it's often considered tasteless and distracting, too much jewelry in the workplace can lead to injuries. Imagine: a large bangle bracelet gets caught on the handle of a coffee pot. Splish. Splash. You get burned, your co-worker gets burned, or a customer gets burned.

If a necktie is part of your uniform, wearing a tie clip is not only a fashion statement, but it will also keep your tie out of the way and out of the food. A universally acceptable length for neckties is waist or belt length.

Hands and Nails

Upon delivering a meal or drink, your hands are center stage. See to it that they look their best for their big performances. Hands must be kept clean, and nails need to be properly manicured. Wash your hands often during your shift, especially after washroom breaks, cigarette breaks, taking out garbage, sneezing, coughing, eating, and handling money.

Studies have found numerous substances on money, some of which are urine, feces, and sperm. Bet you'll think twice now before you lick your fingers while counting money.

Cuts and scrapes, especially on hands, should always remain covered with fresh, secure bandages. Very secure, so bandages don't fall into food or drinks.

 **FYI** ♀ Tip for female servers. Many, if not all, provinces and states have health regulations about nail polish, as do many restaurants. If your boss does allow nail polish, make sure it's freshly applied, not chipped or worn. Also, it's a good idea to lean toward softer colors (French-manicure is attractive and a crowd-pleaser.).

Footwear

Matching socks, run-free stockings and appropriate shoes are all necessary, as footwear is as critical as any other aspect of your uniform.

Be sure to keep your shoes clean, polished and in good condition. From weather soils and slopped sauces to scuffed, worn footwear, your shoes should be kept as clean as the rest of your uniform. Untied or loosely tied laces appear sloppy and, more importantly, are dangerous.

Well-fitted, comfortable work shoes are crucial for servers who spend a lot of time on their feet.

 **FYI** → Tip for all servers. To sidestep smelly feet, wear odor eaters. There are numerous brands on the market from which to choose.

 **FYI →** More about stinky feet. Try sprinkling baking soda or, some prefer, spraying Febreze in shoes between shifts. If you spray them before you go to bed, they'll be dry by morning.

 **FYI →** Still more about stinky feet. Avoid nylon socks because they cause perspiration and often a burning sensation. Try, instead, cotton or wool to wick away perspiration and odor.

 **FYI ♀** Tip for female servers. If you wear nylon stockings and want to avoid foot odor, wear matching ankle socks under your stockings (provided your shoes camouflage them).

 **FYI ♂** Tip for male servers. Don't feel left out by all this girl talk. Count your blessings that you're not a woman. We have to spend a lot more time on grooming to get prepared for work.

Posture

Good posture has many attributes. The way you carry yourself can and will speak volumes about your confidence and health. The way you carry your tray can affect your health and safety. And who looks more attractive: a slumped over, foot-dragging, round-shouldered frump or an upright, sure-footed, self-assured go-getter?

SERVER'S NOTES

Chapter 3

Always be Prepared

Punctuality is a crucial element in being prepared. Being on time is good. Being 10 to 15 minutes early is better. Even if it isn't house policy, which it often is, arriving early has many benefits. Showing up in the nick of time doesn't give you a chance to find out the details of daily specials, to clarify which items, if any, are 86ed, or to look for those darned misplaced pens. But those are the least of the late arrival's troubles. Let's say the restaurant gets busy earlier than anticipated, and one or more of your tables gets seated. Depending on house policy, if another server starts the table(s), they may be allowed, or expected to, keep them, thus minimizing your number of customers and potential tips. There are dozens of other reasons to be on time or early. You're a grown up; figure them out.

Now that you're on time (early), looking great in a uniform, which you probably hate, let's see what else is needed to be all you can be. Sorry about the slogans. I'm not trying to sign you up for Boy Scouts or the Army; but those boys, big and small, have the right idea. Though you probably won't need to purchase a Swiss army knife, there are other tools of the trade that you should always have on hand. You know which of the following are applicable to you and your place of work. If not, ask the boss.

Extra pens

Only the most useless server walks around with one pen.

Then again, there's always some moron with half a dozen pens, none of which actually work, jutting out of a pocket of a filthy apron. Don't let it be you.

FYI → To prevent customers from accidentally pocketing your pens after signing credit card slips or filling out comment cards, give them inexpensive pens with the cap removed. They are much less likely to put a cheap pen with an exposed tip in their pocket.

A server pad or note paper

Whether order pads are supplied by the house or, or not, be sure to have enough paper to last throughout your entire shift.

A billfold, wallet or small purse of some sort

Carrying loose bills in an apron pocket is asking for trouble. If you do cram cash into your pocket in a slovenly manner, I want to know where you work, so I can go in, follow you around, and pick up the fives, tens, and twenties that you drop every time you reach into your pocket to get a quarter or a note pad.

For those of you who haven't read the introduction of this book, I'll reiterate that I have interviewed 100 servers, and 94% of them carry their cash, coupons, gift certificates, debit, and credit card slips in an organized server pouch of some sort.

Keeping cash in denominational order, heads facing the same way (bank style) helps to eliminate errors when making change, especially in dimly lit dining rooms or bars.

A float

Few restaurants have cashiers to collect bill payments. The prepared server carries $20, $30, $40 (your choice) in small bills and coin to make change for their customers. Even if the house doesn't expect you to carry a float, it's a good idea, in case a customer is in a hurry to get change, in case the cash register is short of small bills, in case the cashier isn't available when you need him/her.

A server's corkscrew

...and the know-how to present, open and pour wine properly. You can pick up a server's corkscrew for less than five dollars (a co-worker of mine spent eight dollars on his, where another dug hers out of a bargain bin at a dollar store. I just chitchat with the wine reps., and they usually give me one.). We'll go into wine knowledge and service more in the chapter entitled *'Wining and Dining' (Chapter 11)*

You've taken the time to make sure you're prepared, now take the time to make sure your section is prepared.

Check your section at the beginning of your shift before your tables get seated. Start your inspection at the ceiling and work your way down. Are lampshades dusted? Do any light bulbs need replacing? Inspect cutlery, glassware, side plates, centerpieces, table tents for cleanliness (food particles, water spots, fingerprints, etc.). If you're in a smoking section (if your establishment still has a smoking section), be sure ashtrays are not simply on the tables, but also that they are clean and dry.

Table condiments are often overlooked. This refers to cleanliness and contents. Keep condiments full. If your restaurant uses sugar/sweetener packets, make sure they're not only well stocked, but also, that they aren't beat up, torn open, half empty or coffee stained. As for cleanliness, have you ever picked up a ketchup bottle only to find it caked with crusty food particles? Yuck! Have you ever tried to grip a salt shaker but couldn't because it squirted out of your hand like a wet bar of soap? Double yuck! So, wipe/clean/inspect everything in your section, starting with the overhead lampshade and then working your way down to the table, napkins, cutlery, glassware, side plates, rollups, cups and saucers, condiments, table tents, benches and chairs.

Be sure the tables are clean, top and bottom; be sure there is not gum or anything sticky on the underside of the table. If your place of employment uses table clothes, be sure they are not soiled or wrinkled. Place the cloth in the center of the table so that the sides drape evenly off each side of the table. With linen (or any cloth, for that matter), put the seam on the underside.

Lastly, give the floor a visual once-over and push chairs in neatly. Granted, we're not cleaners or sweepers, but it is in your best interest to take a couple of minutes out of your busy life to ensure that your customers feel at home in your section. Atmosphere is a part of any dining experience. After all, you don't want your customers focusing on an unsanitary, messy restaurant, when they should be focusing on your amazing serving abilities, and more importantly, your tip.

So, to recap:

- ✓ You show up a few minutes before your shift.
- ✓ You and your uniform look professional and presentable.
- ✓ You are armed with all the necessary tools of the trade.
- ✓ Your section is immaculate and inviting.
- ✓ Last but not least, don't forget to bring your smile.

SERVER'S NOTES

Chapter 4

Service with a Smile ☺

It takes 64 muscles to frown and only 13 to smile.

Or is it 27 to frown and 6 to smile?

Whatever.

The point is, servers must maintain a sense of humor, give friendly, enthusiastic service and always display grace under pressure.

You'd think smiling was a given; however, to the dismay of many unfortunate patrons, too many servers forget the importance of a simple smile. Who among us has suffered the brunt of a server's surly expression or crusty mood? The answer to that question is alarming.

As stated in the introduction, to get an accurate response, I randomly surveyed 1000 customers over a period of nearly five years. And the survey says, "A whopping 99.3% of customers from a wide variety of ages, races, financial classes, and ethnicities have had their dining experience hampered because of their server's demeanor."

That means, only 7 out of a possible 1000 have not been annoyed by a server who didn't smile.

Glenda, server of twenty-eight years, laughed as she explained her theory on the disposition of employees from institutions like the Post Office or the DMV. "They're obviously not working for tips."

About your personal life, it's a good idea to keep it to yourself. People go out to dinner for more than the obvious hunger/nutrition reasons. Some go to get away from their troubles. The point? If they don't want to think about their own problems, they certainly don't want to hear about yours. Chatting can be a good thing, but not when you're chatting about your woes. Do not let customers hear you moaning and cursing about your recent breakup, your hangover, or that stupid hairdresser who gave you the blanking-blank cut.

When you clock-in, it's time to turn off your problems and do your job. Most bosses would prefer you to call in sick, rather than have you mope around their restaurant, depressing their customers. If a restaurant is the stage, then you are the star. Would a star go on stage out of character? I think not.

Don't forget that a positive attitude needn't be reserved for customers. Be sure to save some for your co-workers. My mom always told me "You catch more flies with honey than you do with vinegar."

Knowing the importance of a smile is only the beginning. You need to know much, much more.

Chapter 5

Know Your Stuff

There's more to serving than knowing how to tie an apron, make change, and fetch.

> Curious Customer, "What's the soup du jour?"
> Simpleton Server, "That's French for soup of the day."

Many types, or styles, of service exist. Among the many are French or tableside, English, Russian, Gueridon, modern, buffet, plate or American and Butler-style. Old-school traditional rules of the various styles of service tend to be combined or revised by individual establishments more often than not. Therefore, to explicitly define any of the above would be moot. Since there are such an abundance of opinions on presentation, how cutlery should be laid out, serving from the left and clearing from the right, and so forth, it is best to follow house policy wherever you work. Otherwise, you're only asking to make your job harder.

'How hard can it be?' or 'How much do you have to know to be a server?' Only people who've never done our job would have the audacity to ask questions like that.

To both of those questions, I say, "Huh!"

We, as servers, need to (should) know as much as any other employee in any other business. We need to know as many details as possible about all that the establishment has to offer.

We need to be able to thoroughly describe and answer every possible question about:

- Food
- Beer and Draught
- Drinks
- Soft Drinks
- Wine
- Coffee and Tea
- Basic Serving Procedures
- Prices
- The Establishment
- "Hero products"

Food

➤ Know your food preparation: minced, shredded, pickled, pureed, julienne, fricasseed, smoked, etc. (The calamari is marinated in milk to tenderize it.).
➤ Know basic ingredients (Then it is dusted with flour, seasoned with fresh garlic and a dash of lemon pepper.).
➤ How are foods cooked: baked, barbecued, basted, boiled, braised, broiled, deep fried, pan fried, flambéed, grilled, poached, roasted, steamed, smoked, sautéed, seared, simmered, stewed, toasted? (Today's vegetable is a medley of garden fresh broccoli, cauliflower, and baby carrots, steamed with just a whisper of butter.)
➤ Know house standards for varying degrees of doneness for meat. You should be able to explain using color and temperature descriptions, i.e.:
  - Rare - *seared outside with a cool red center.*
  - Medium Rare - *warmish with a mostly red center*
  - Medium - *warm with bright pink throughout*
  - Medium Well - *hot, brown with a thin strip of light*

pink through the center.
- **Well Done** - *hot, brown throughout (no pink at all)*

Some lesser heard styles of cooking meat are:
- **Blue Rare** - *outer grill marks are barely visible, while the inner color is quite red (blue) and the meat is cold.*
- **Pittsburg style, Boston Burn, Chicago Style** - *are all terms that refer to charring the outside of the meat with high heat. The internal temperature can still be cooked to order (to any doneness mentioned above).*

The above are merely examples; check with your house for their guidelines.

➢ Know your portion sizes. Do not use obscure hand gestures indicating that something is "about this big". Know, for example, the number of ounces (Our surf and turf dinner consists of an eight-ounce center cut, sirloin steak and a 5 to 6-ounce lobster tail).

➢ Are there any seasonal items on your menu? If so, are they currently in stock? You need to know which fruits, vegetables, seafood, etc. are seasonal and when they are and aren't available.

➢ If any of the items on the menu are "market priced" stay abreast of the prices (Lobster and crab are often listed this way on menus.).

➢ Accompaniments. Make sure you know what comes with what (Your dinner comes with a choice of baked potato, french fries, home fries, or mashed potatoes and vegetables.).

➢ Know house policy on substitutions (You can trade the complimentary house salad for a Greek salad for only $1.25).

> Five Easy Pieces - I'd like to take this opportunity to tell you about one of my favorite restaurant/movie scenes. In the 1970 movie entitled Five Easy Pieces, starring Jack Nicholson and Karen Black (among others), Nicholson and a truck stop waitress get into a heated discussion about menu substitutions.
>
> Nicholson asks for toast; and to his request the waitress tells him that they don't serve toast.
>
> "What do you mean, you don't serve toast?" Nicholson asks.
>
> "We don't serve toast," she retorts, firmly.
>
> Nicholson then goes into a ranting rampage about the fact that they have bread for sandwiches, and they have a toaster, so why won't they make him an order of toast?
>
> Still, the waitress won't budge on policy.
>
> Alas, Nicholson orders a chicken salad sandwich. He wants it toasted. He also wants her to hold the lettuce and hold the mayo. Finally he tells her to hold the chicken (between her knees) and just bring him the toast he so desperately wanted in the first place.
>
> If you're not smiling at this point, rent the movie. That classic Nicholson delivery will send you into side-splitting laughter.

- ➢ Know all of the above about apps.
- ➢ Know all of the above about sides.
- ➢ Know all of the above about desserts.
- ➢ Know which appetizers, sides, and desserts go good with which entrées (Greek Salad as a starter for souvlaki, steak with sautéed mushrooms, follow up pork chops with apple pie...don't forget to offer à la mode.).

Beer and Draught

Beer dates back thousands of years BC, as far back as the brilliant, ancient Egyptians, who consumed more beer than all other beverages combined. So you can imagine that beer has evolved by leaps and bounds over the centuries.

➢ Do your homework; *beer and draught* aren't as simple as they sound. There's lager, dark lager, light, ale, pale ale, dark ale, Pilsner, port, stout, bock, bitter, ice, dry, cream ale, honey brown, rice beer, wheat, brown, red, amber and blonde ales to name a few. Don't even get us started on all the microbreweries that are popping up all over the world.

➢ Speaking of the rest of the world, be sure to know which beers are domestic and which are imported and from where.

Molson products ▶ Canada	Schlitz ▶ U.S.A.
Heineken ▶ Holland	Bass ▶ England
Fosters ▶ Australia	Becks ▶ Germany
Pilsner Urquell ▶ Czech Republic	Sapporo ▶ Japan
Stella Artois ▶ Belgium	Moretti ▶ Italy
Steinlager ▶ New Zealand	Harp ▶ Ireland
Tsing Tao ▶ China	Corona ▶ Mexico

- Know what's on tap.
- What sizes of draught do you serve?
- Know the quality importance of serving draught promptly.
- What bottled beers are available?
- Do you carry a non-alcohol beer?
- Chase a shot of whiskey with a beer, and what do you call it? A boilermaker.
- Mix a citrus soft drink or ginger ale with beer, and you've created a shandy.
- Beer and tomato juice…a red-eye.
- If a customer orders a "black and tan" do you know what that is? A "black and tan" is a mixture of dark and pale beer such as port and Pilsner or stout and bitter.

Drinks

- Know names and ingredients of basic drinks (highballs, cocktails, aperitifs, shooters).
- Know well/house brands of liquor.
- Know premium brands of liquor.
- Know which liqueurs are stocked.
- Know recipes for house specialty drinks.

- Know the difference between single malt and blended scotches, and know which you carry.
- Know whether drinks are traditionally served straight up, on the rocks or blended. And which of these should you ask how they'd like it.
- Know proper garnishes for all drinks. Lemon? Lime? Orange? Pineapple? Cherry? Salt or sugar rim? Etc.
- A dirty martini is simply a martini with olive juice added.

> Puzzled Patron, "Do you serve a shrimp cocktail?"
>
> Worthless Waiter, "Sorry, we don't have a liquor license."

- Know the proper glassware (i.e. straight up Grand Marnier goes in a snifter [a heated snifter is a nice touch], Black Russian goes in a rocks glass).

Soft Drinks

- Know your soft drinks.
- Know if your restaurant carries Coke products, Pepsi products, or perhaps a lesser-known brand.
- Are there free refills on soft drinks?
- Do the refills apply to tap pop only, or are milk and juices included?
- Does your establishment carry homogenized, 2%, or skimmed milk?
- Do you have chocolate milk?
- Do you have milkshakes?
- Do you have ice cream floats?
- What kinds of mocktails (virgin/non-alcohol drinks) are available?
- What's in a kiddie cocktail/Shirley Temple?

- ➤ What kinds of juices are stocked?
- ➤ Are the juices all natural, or do they have more additives and preservatives than fruits and vegetables?
- ➤ Are you serving name brands like Heinz, Mott's and Allen's, or are you serving a no-name or lesser known brand?
- ➤ What kind of bottled waters do you carry? Do you have carbonated? Sparkling? Still? Where is it from?
- ➤ Is your iced tea pre-sweetened or unsweetened?

FYI ➔ Long time servers have noticed that generally, Americans prefer unsweetened iced tea, whereas Canadians prefer pre-sweetened iced tea. Don't forget to garnish with a lemon wedge or slice.

Wine

- ➤ Know your wine list.
- ➤ Know house wines.
- ➤ Know domestic wines.
- ➤ Know imported and where they're from.
- ➤ Know proper wine glasses.
- ➤ Know which wines can be ordered by the glass, carafe or bottle and which can be purchased only by bottles.

- Know the sizes of the bottles.
- Know how to present, open, and serve wines.
- Know which wines will enhance which foods. This can take a great deal of homework.
- As promised, we'll go into more details in the Chapter 11 entitled *'Wining and Dining'*.

Coffee
- Know what kind of coffee you're serving (100% Colombian, Venezuela/Cochabamba blend).

- Know if you're serving a bottomless cup of coffee.
- Do you serve brewed de-caffeinated?
- Do you offer cappuccino, espresso, latte, mocha, etc.?
- What kind of tea do you serve?

- Do you have any herbal teas? What brand? Flavors?
- Do you have hot chocolate?
- Do you have low calorie sweetener? If so, what kind?
- What kind of cream is available? Table cream? Half and half?
- Be prepared to list and describe a variety of liqueur coffees.

Basic Serving Procedures and Etiquette
- When placing a meal in front of a customer, always situate the plate so that the main attraction (typically the protein: meat, poultry, seafood, whatever) is closest to the customer (at six o'clock).
- Speaking of time: Although there are many ways to set a

table, one detail seems to be agreed upon. When placing a coffee cup on a saucer, the handle should point to four o'clock. If you are able to ascertain that the customer is left-handed, turn the handle to eight o'clock.

- 94% of the interviewed servers also agree that when setting a table, the knife blade should be facing inward toward the fork.
- If you serve a knife on the plate, do so on the right-hand side.
- If a customer uses the wrong utensil (dinner fork for salad or steak knife for butter), do not comment or correct them. Do not draw attention or embarrass them. Instead, replace the missing cutlery discreetly, while clearing for the next course.
- When refilling coffee cups, remove the cup from the table by the saucer, refill far enough from the customer so that you do not risk spilling, then replace it cautiously returning the handle to the four o'clock position.
- A similar technique should be used for refilling water glasses. Grasp the glass by the base, pour clear from the customer, and then replace the glass carefully.
- If you pour a beer for a customer, always tilt the glass to avoid too much foam. And don't fill the glass to the top. That way if they like foam, they can top up the glass themselves.
- When serving food to booths or tables that only have one possible pivot point, serve the farthest people first. For customer on the right side of the booth, serve the closest person with your right hand and the farthest with your left, to avoid elbowing the closer person in the head.
- Keep thumbs as close as possible to the outer edge of the plate and away from food and garnishes.
- Tables should be kept free of crumbs. Use a crumber (scraper), crumb brush or napkin to brush crumbs off the table and onto a small plate (not your hand or the floor).

- 👍 See Chapter 11, *'Wining and Dining'* for proper wine serving procedures.
- 👍 Use coasters or beverage napkins where applicable.
- 👍 Clear table and change ashtrays before delivering food. Place a clean dry ashtray on top of the dirty one (this prevents ashes from flying around); pick up both ashtrays and remove. Be sure to place a clean ashtray back on the table. Never touch a customer's cigarette. If it's sitting in the ashtray that you want to change, ask the customer to remove it.
- 👍 Know how to pronounce all words on the menu and how to interpret them.
- 👍 Even in this day of equality, serving ladies first is almost always appreciated.
- 👍 Serve the 'host' last (the person who's paying or who made the reservation), if you can tell who that is.
- 👍 When clearing plates, try to clear all plates at the same time, if possible. Unless a customer asks or pushes their plate to the edge of the table, wait until their dining companions are finished before removing empty plates or offering to pack leftovers to go.
- 👍 Do not stack dirty plates in front of the customers.
- 👍 When providing any service for your customers, do not reach too closely in front of them any more than necessary. Try to be as unobtrusive as possible.
- 👍 As business slows down, the number of servers is usually slowly reduced. Cutting, closing or phasing are three different terminologies for this practice. At this point, remaining servers' sections are then enlarged, or some sections of the restaurant are closed off.

Prices

- From drinks and apps., to sides and desserts, strong servers know prices.
- Stay abreast of prices and details of changeable daily specials.
- Keep tabs on market prices where applicable.
- Did you know that some countries, provinces, and states have different taxes on alcohol than on food? Ask the boss or check the tax laws for your geographic location. This knowledge is valuable when serving cash and carry drinks or if the power goes out or the computer crashes and you have to prepare bills manually.

About the Establishment

Don't forget to stay abreast of:

- Operating hours
- Holiday hours
- Daily specials
- Weekly/monthly specials
- Daily features
- Soup of the day
- Catch of the day
- Daily vegetable
- Early bird specials
- Senior's discounts
- Upcoming promotions
- House policy on recycling
- Parking availability
- Special events
- Entertainment
- Cover charges
- Etc.

"Hero products"

➢ What are some of the best selling items? What is the establishment known for: jumbo shrimp cocktail, prime rib, Margaritas, home-made cheesecake?

Many old expressions are true, but you can bet that the old expression "nobody likes a know-it-all" doesn't apply to your customers.

How, you may ask, can you be a know-it-all?

- Self educate.
- Ask questions.
- Read.
- Ask a trainer.
- Ask a manager.
- Watch and learn. Observe fellow servers. Pay attention to what employees in other departments are doing (cooks, bartenders, etc.).
- Sample foods at staff meetings (if available), before or after your shift, or on your day off.
- Try drinks that you aren't familiar with. Who says learning can't be fun?
- Ask to borrow a menu and/or training manual and begin studying immediately, preferably before your first shift.
- Lastly, you don't have to memorize all of the above. Feel free to keep cheat-sheets in your pocket. If it helps you learn the trade there's nothing wrong with taking notes.

SERVER'S NOTES

PART TWO

LEARNING THE TRADE

In This Part

Chapter 6: Take notes

Chapter 7: Teamwork - Do Unto Others

Chapter 8: Economizing Steps + Maximum Efficiency = Maximum Tips

Chapter 9: Making the Boss Sit up and Take Notice

Chapter 10: Sell! Sell! Sell!

Chapter 11: Wining and Dining

Wine Glossary

SERVER'S NOTES

Chapter 6

Take Notes ✍

The phone rings. Someone wants to book a reservation. That's when the note taking starts. All details must be put in writing: name, date, time, number of people, phone number, and it doesn't hurt to ask if they're celebrating a special occasion.

Provided all goes well with the reservation, the next step is to serve the customers when they arrive in your section. Unless the house has a policy against the writing of orders (which 87% of the surveyed servers think is insane), please put pen to paper and avoid unnecessary blunders. Customers aren't expecting you to be the Amazing Kreskin, just the person who brings them what they order. Exactly what they order. A martini is not a vodka martini. Medium well is not medium rare.

By all means, if you can get through weeks at a time without writing at least partial orders, and not make mistakes because of it, go for it. But be honest with yourself, if not me; can you ... really? I hate to be skeptical, but I've seen and heard a lot of horror stories about servers who 'memorize' orders. Again, if you can do it, kudos to you. You are a rarity.

You needn't write all orders in longhand; use abbreviations. If the house doesn't have any standards in place, make up your own abbr. i.e.:

With = /
Triple Fudge Brownie Surprise = fudge
French fries = FF

Fettuccini Alfredo = fet alf   Sautéed mushrooms = mush
Strawberry Daiquiri = S daq   onion rings = O rings
Tequila straight up = teq ↑

Where hand written guest checks or hand written kitchen or bar orders are expected, write neatly and concisely. This is rarely seen in our age of computers, still not a bad idea to write clearly even if no one else sees your notes to avoid errors.

To save a lot of paperwork and hassle you may want to ask, up front, whether they would like one bill or separate bills? If you're approaching an obvious husband and wife or a small family (mommy, daddy and two small children), you needn't ask. However, larger parties of two or more adult couples often prefer separate bills.

FYI → 74% of the interviewed servers make better tips from separate bills. Reason: large bills cause what's known as "sticker shock". 15% of a tab worth hundreds of dollars appears steep. With several small totals, a higher percent per bill seems more affordable.

Large corporate eating and drinking establishments and food chains usually have a system for organization of seat numbers. Independent operations often leave the organizing up to the employees. If the house has set standards, follow them. If, for example, the house doesn't have designated pivot points, make up your own. And stick to them. By doing this you minimize the unorganized act of *raffling off* dinners and drinks upon delivery, meaning...you shouldn't have to ask, "Who ordered the chicken?" Based on the location on your note pad, you'll instinctively know where everything goes. If another server is helping to deliver your meals, be sure they know your pivot point and seat numbers. It is to your advantage to work as a team.

Chapter 7

Teamwork - Do Unto Others
(as you would have them do unto you)

In this chapter we'll discuss the importance of teamwork amongst restaurant employees.

Starting from the moment the customer enters the establishment, teamwork is essential. If the person in charge of seating tables is not available, greet and seat patrons immediately. Never make a customer wait.

First come, first serve does not always apply to you and your co-workers, however. The laws of the road should not apply if an empty-handed person gets to a doorway before a person carrying a full tray. Same goes if you have a beer on a small bar tray, and someone else has a large kitchen tray with four dinners steaming above their shoulder. Back off. Always give the 'right of way' to the bigger load.

If another server's customer flags you down to ask for something, whether it be a glass of water, a clean fork, another bottle of wine, or whatever, get them what they need or tell their server what they need. Make another server look good, and hopefully they'll do the same for you sometime. If you're extremely busy and someone else's customer wants descriptions of every appetizer on the menu, it can be acceptable to let them know that you'll tell/get their server. But be forewarned, no one likes an indifferent server with a snooty tone. Be polite, and go get their server immediately. If you don't know who their server is, go find out. Don't ask the customer who's waiting on them or you'll look clueless. Besides, it's not their job to know their server's name. They're there to relax, not to be quizzed.

And for heaven's sake, if you deliver someone else's food or drinks, finish the job.

- Know where you're going and who gets what.
- Do a quality check to make sure everything is okay, or inform the appropriate server that the item(s) have been delivered so that they can check the table.
- Make sure the customers have everything they ordered. Pay attention to extra sides, requested garnishes, or special orders.
- Be sure to bring appropriate accompaniments: sauces, sides, a cold glass for a bottle of beer, etc.
- If it seems appropriate, offer to bring more drinks, refill soft drinks, or suggest wine, and then tell their server what is needed.
- Remove any unnecessary clutter from the table: plates, glasses, cream for coffee, etc.
- Smile. Be nice.
- Basically, do the same for someone else's table that you would do for your own. Do unto others, help them make great tips now, and they'll help you later.

Sidework

I can't think of a better time to address one of our top ten server's pet peeves regarding other servers. The topic in question is side work. Nothing ticks off other servers more than having to do all the clean up, while a few lazy hotshots line their pockets with tips without lifting a finger to clean up behind themselves.

You know the type, the people who pack up a doggie bag and leave the empty plates sitting on the counter. The same slackers who take the last after-dinner mint and don't refill the bowl. The careless co-workers who spill things and don't clean up or ask someone to help them.

Sure, we all know that customers and tips are our priorities. However, when you aren't busy with your customers:

- Clear, tidy, and wipe work areas and countertops.
- Stock service stations. Make sure there are creamers, sugar caddies, coffee filters, under liners, mints, billfolds, teaspoons, coffee cups, side plates, glassware, etc.
- Take a pot make a pot. This rule is self-explanatory. As long as there are people to drink it, there should be a pot of coffee brewing. If you take a pot that just finished brewing, make a pot for your fellow servers.
- Shine cutlery.
- Fold napkins/do rollups.
- Refill water pitchers.
- Stock ice.
- Slice lemons.
- Etc.

As much as personality, style, organization, and efficiency are all essential components for an accomplished server, the importance of background work must not be overlooked. Without ongoing preparation and side work, you will not be seen as a tip-worthy server. Be kind to the back of house staff as well. The chefs/cooks, prep people, and even the dishwashers. Especially the dishwashers! Think about it: being a dish-pig is the most thankless, disgusting job in the business. As with any other employee, dishwashers must be treated with the same respect that you deserve.

> Deirdre, server of 21 years, felt sorry for the dishwashers who, she realized, were stuck with the most repulsive job in the house. Therefore, she began offering to bring them cold soft drinks or hot coffees. In return, they separated her silverware, stacked her plates and even carried bus-bins for her when the bussers were not available. Thanks to them, Deirdre saved steps and was able to spend more time with her tipping customers.

It's all about habits versus routines. The word habit almost always comes with negative connotations. Routine, contrarily, is a positive word. So break bad habits, and get into a good routine.

Now that we've established the do unto others policy applies to back of house staff as well as front of house staff, let us not forget it is also valid where your customers are concerned. Personality counts as much as efficiency does.

Chapter 8

Economizing Steps + Maximum Efficiency = Maximum Tips

One of the primary ways to save the treads on your shoes is to always obey the "Full Hands In...Full Hands Out" rule. If you're going into the kitchen to drop something off...bring out something else. Never walk around empty handed. Bring food to a table...take away empty glasses. Take dirty dishes to the dish pit...check the line to see if there's food that needs to be run. Take a bus-bin back to the kitchen...bring out a pot of coffee to top up your tables' cups. Pour coffee for your customers...come away from the table with empty wine glasses. Get it?

Run your section; don't let your section run you. Meaning, don't give anyone an opportunity to ask you to make three treks to the kitchen or bar, when you can get them everything they need in one trip. It's easier than it sounds. If one person at a four-top asks for another drink, be sure to ask the other three if they would like a refill. "Can I bring another round?"

Get the entire order before you try to place the order. Would you like soup, salad or juice? Greek, Caesar or tossed? What kind of dressing? Would you prefer the dressing on the salad or on the side? What kind of juice would you like? How would you like your eggs? Would you like your sandwich on white or brown bread? Toasted or plain? Mashed, baked or fries? How would you like your steak cooked? Describe how their steak will look (i.e. "Our medium well is hot and brownish with a light pink strip down the center."). These questions are all pointless, or not in your vocabulary, if you don't know your stuff. Knowing your stuff is a key factor in conserving energy.

In time you will come to know cooking/preparation times. After a while, you will get a feel for how long the kitchen takes to prepare different dishes. For example, if you've ordered pasta dishes or specials, they shouldn't take long; therefore, you should check the kitchen sooner to see if your order is up. If, on the other hand, you've ordered a well done rack of lamb or complicated dishes, you can probably focus on other things and check the kitchen later. Alertness and experience will teach you how to identify when the kitchen is weeded and meals will take longer. How many orders are pending has a large bearing on your timing. Different chefs/cooks also have different paces as well as styles; therefore, who's cooking will be another factor to take into consideration.

Carrying Plates

You'll hear of numerous "proper" techniques for carrying plates. There are innumerable ways to carry multiple plates; all of them up to interpretation. Your individual style and panache will be your own. The ability to carry numerous plates will save countless steps. All of the interviewed servers agreed that practicing at home with paper plates is a great idea and can be quite entertaining. As time passes, carrying more plates will become second nature.

As mentioned earlier, one rule (of thumb) that is not up to interpretation is the matter of keeping thumbs as close as possible to the outer edge of the plate and away from food and garnishes.

Pick up the plates in the opposite order that you intend to serve them. Meaning, your serving hand will have the first plate in it, and plate two should be the next most easily accessible and then plate three, and so on.

Carrying Food Trays

When loading and carrying food trays the server should follow certain basic rules:

- Use a tray that is clean, top and bottom.
- For trays without non-slip surfaces like cork, placing a damp cloth on the tray will reduce slippage.
- Never overload a tray. Only place as much on the tray as you can handle comfortably.
- Load heavier items in the center of the tray.
- Leave space between hot and cold items.
- Keep soups, gravies, sauces and liquids on a level surface.
- Point handles, spouts, cutlery and any protruding objects toward the center of the tray.
- When stacking items, do so cautiously.
- Balancing the load is a main priority.
- Bend at the knees while keeping your back straight, when picking up and putting down a tray.
- Place your shoulder under the tray to lift; do not hoist the tray

up onto your shoulder.
- ➤ Your hand should be at the center of the tray.
- ➤ Use your shoulder to help balance.
- ➤ Stack underliners separately on the tray to save space.
- ➤ Uncovered foods are to be kept away from your hair.
- ➤ Use your free hand to help balance and to carry a tray stand.
- ➤ Always carry trays close to the body to avoid accidents.
- ➤ Keep your range of view as open as possible. Obstructing your view with a tray can lead to tripping over purses, dragging coats, or even small children.
- ➤ Be sure that all dinners are delivered to the table at the same time. If you cannot carry everything, ask someone to follow you with the remainder of the order, or go back immediately to retrieve the rest of the food (no detours).

Drink Trays

Drink trays are loaded and treated similarly, only on a smaller scale. Clustering glasses and bottles in the center of a drink tray can help with balance, as can using the flat palm of the hand rather than fingertips to carry. As you remove items, wriggle your tray fingers slightly to accommodate the ever-changing shift of weight.

As you deliver items to a table, be sure not to mix up orders. Let's say, for instance, you happen to have two steak dinners at the same table (one medium rare and one medium) it doesn't hurt to say the order aloud as you're placing the food on the table. (This is not to be mistaken with asking or raffling.) When the customers hear you, they'll either figure you're thinking out loud (which is fine), or they'll tell you 'the other steak' is theirs. In case of the latter, you simply switch the plates, and you've just avoided a minimum of two trips to the kitchen (one to return the wrong steaks that the customers had to cut into to find out they were wrong and one to bring out the proper orders).

There are also countless small things you can do to help budget your time. A few time-budgeting techniques are listed below:

- Try to get app. orders with first drink orders. This will save you steps and add an extra sale to the bill. Simply point out the appetizer list and suggest at least two different items. If they appear interested, say, "I can order your appetizers now, then we can discuss your entrées later."
- Sell wine by the bottle or carafe instead of by the glass. Make a larger sale and save extra trips with one simple suggestion.
- Bring steak sauce, ketchup, clarified butter for shellfish, or other possibly needed condiments with or before the appropriate entrées.
- Since more people prefer milk instead of cream in their tea, you can save steps by automatically bringing milk with tea or by asking the customer what they prefer. In fact, many enjoy lemon in tea; therefore asking would probably be the best way to save extra steps.
- Take after-dinner drink orders and dessert orders at the same time. Be sure to deliver them likewise.

Servers who waste steps end up with a sweaty brow, sore feet, and are always in the weeds.

Servers who know how to economize steps are always in control, pull in lots of tips, and make the boss sit up and take notice.

SERVER'S NOTES

Chapter 9

Making the Boss Sit Up and Take Notice

Words like "Sorry, that's not my section" should never come out of your mouth.

If there's time to lean, there's time to clean.

Full hands in, full hands out.

Waste not, want not.

I know what you're thinking. You think this is starting to sound more like a boss than a fellow server wrote it. Think again.

Allow me to elaborate. Let's start with "Sorry, that's not my section." Granted, each server is typically responsible for one section. But that's only the smaller picture. In the bigger picture, the boss is responsible for all of the sections. All of the customers are the boss's customers. Therefore, if you are polite and helpful to everyone, whether they're in your section or not, you will definitely please the boss.

As for "If there's time to lean, there's time to clean" there are many reasons to putter. Cleaning and stocking as you work will save time at the end of your shift. When you keep busy, time flies. Idle hands don't make money for you or the establishment. Although our hourly wage is meager, we are being paid to work, not to lean on the bar and flirt with the bartender.

"Full hands in, full hands out" keeps things organized, stocked and prepared. As mentioned above, when your hands are full on your way into the kitchen and on your way out, the boss will see that you're a worker, not a slacker.

"Waste not, want not" simply refers to being cautious and frugal.

Using caution is obvious in a business where we're surrounded by so many breakables. Keep your hands clean and dry to avoid slippage. Never carry oversized loads. Don't stack breakables too high. Overall, use common sense.

As far as being frugal is concerned, some areas to be thrifty in are:

➢ Labor cost.

Remove extra place settings when seating tables. This is one way to save labor, as the dishwashers will not have to wash dishes that would otherwise not need to be cleaned. It also saves the bussers or servers the time they would spend putting away the dishes and polishing the cutlery.

➢ Food cost.

Save on food cost by putting lemon wedges in water glasses only when customers ask for it.

➢ Utilities.

- When not in use, turn off coffee burners and other electric appliances and switches.
- Keep heat and air conditioning at a reasonable temperature, and ensure doors and windows are closed properly.
- Don't leave water running. Turn taps off completely after use.

Supplies.

Believe it or not, the biggest waste in restaurants consists of items thoughtlessly discarded into the garbage. Items such as:

- full creamers
- unopened butter pats
- linen napkins
- unused paper napkins
- small bowls and plates
- and the most costly, worst culprit…cutlery (accidentally thrown out while scraping plates or buried under serviettes)

Pretend you're the boss or that the restaurant is your home. Would you be wasteful or careless at home, where you are paying the bills?

Servers are a dime a dozen, but one efficient server is priceless.

One thing that can't be stressed enough is whether you are saving money or making money for the restaurant, the boss can't help but sit up and take notice. It's all about respect!

The introduction promised to share the secret of how to get better tip shifts and bigger sections. Well, there couldn't be a better time to unveil the answer to that secret. Aside from the obvious things like respect, dedication and efficiency, the answer is:

Communication!

Let's say they keep slotting you in for small sections because you're new. If that's the case, make sure you're seen doing an amazing job in those puny sections. And if that doesn't do the trick, let the boss know that you're looking forward to getting into larger sections. "I wouldn't mind trying my hand at the (high volume) section by the windows." Or, use a more confident approach. "Give me a shot at the VIP section by the fireplace, and I promise you won't be disappointed."

Maybe your problem is that you are repeatedly scheduled for slower shifts. If so, let the boss know you are available and eager to work the busier shifts. "I'm keeping my Saturday nights open in case you need me." Or, use a more confident approach. "I know you need strong servers for Saturday nights. I'm strong and available." But be prepared to back any statements or promises you make. Don't sell the boss something you can't deliver. If you say you can do something and then fail to deliver, you'll be back to small sections and slow shifts so fast it'll make your head spin.

Speaking of selling, another sure way to make the boss sit up and take notice is to Sell! Sell! Sell!

Chapter 10

Sell! Sell! Sell!

There are two kinds of servers:

1) order takers

and

2) salespeople.

In case you don't get where this is going, you want to be the latter.

"Can I get you anything to drink besides water?"

AAARG! Such questions induce a loud scream inside my head, as they should in any salesperson. What is that: down-selling?

Servers often ask, "Why should I knock myself out to make more money for the boss?"

Hopefully, you aren't misguided enough to think that the boss is the only one making money on your sales. Think about it, customers typically base their gratuity on a percentage of the total of the bill. This leads us to the obvious: for every dollar you make for the house, you make a percentage of that dollar for yourself.

Servers receive no tips for tap water. Try up-selling instead. One of the main focuses of a foodservice salesperson is "suggestive selling".

This does not mean "pushy" sales tactics. By using a soft selling approach, you need only use suggestive sales. And in using **$UGGESTIVE ALE**, you are not only expecting to receive a sale, but you are also giving much in return for that potential sale. You are giving your customers:

Sound recommendations
Understanding
Guidance
Genuine concern
Educated endorsements
Timesaving pointers
Individual focus
Variety, variation, versatility
Economic offers and options
Sharable selections

Specific ingredients
Appetizing descriptions
Lasting impressions
Enticing paring options
Special attention for specific needs

Who better to provide all of these things to the customer than you, the person who knows the menu inside and out!

There are many ways to increase sales if a server is on the ball. When it comes to up-selling, be creative.

> Suggestive up-selling tip: Let's say someone asks for an iced tea, ask if they want the bartender's specialty Long Island iced tea (Be sure to explain the difference). Now that's an up-sell!

Laugh at Ronald McDonald if you like, but "Would you like fries with that?" is a perfect example of suggestive sales.

Entrée sales are almost always a given. However, there are at least 8 add-ons (items other than entrées) that you can suggest (sell) to your customers.

1) Suggest (sell) drinks
2) Suggest (sell) appetizers
3) Suggest (sell) wine
4) Suggest (sell) sides
5) Suggest (sell) drink refills
6) Suggest (sell) desserts
7) Suggest (sell) after-dinner drinks
8) Suggest (sell) coffees

Affective salespeople can make commissions (tips) come as easy as if you were simply going into the backyard and harvesting cash from your very own money tree.

In the following pages, we'll go over these sales and up-sale opportunities one by one.

1) **Drinks:**

- Be prepared to explain recipes and give enticing descriptions for house specialty drinks.
- Suggest premium liquors for mixed drinks. (If a customer asks for a scotch and soda, offer a single malt scotch.)
- Offer premium liquors in cocktails, as well. (Suggest Beefeater Martinis or Crown Royal in a Whiskey Sour.)
- Recommend discounted drinks if applicable. This is the volume approach of selling more for less.
- Offer "house size" or double shots. Many establishments offer a discounted, or lower priced, second shot. Take advantage of this opportunity to score an extra sale and give your customer a deal.
- If a customer says, "I'll just have water" ask if they'd like bottled water (still or sparkling), soda water, tonic water, or tap water.
- Use lots of ice in alcoholic drinks. Drinks with extra ice will not only be colder, but customers will taste the alcohol (know they're getting their money's worth). Plus, with less mix they'll be ready for another drink sooner.
- Use thicker straws or two straws to keep drinks flowing faster.
- On the other hand, to save steps, use less ice and thinner straws for free refill, soft drinks.
- For coffee or tea drinkers, offer a liqueur on the side or an alternative: liqueur coffee, tea, cappuccino, espresso, mocha, etc.
- Be sure to offer your customers "another" drink or another round of drinks.
- Keep in mind, alcohol stimulates hunger. Selling a cocktail or two up front can make selling appetizers easier for you.

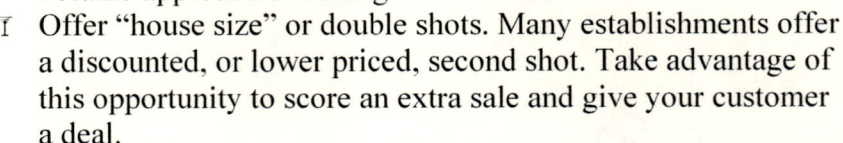

Veering away from restaurants for a moment, let's go into a different atmosphere: bars. Taverns, pubs, neighborhood saloons, watering holes, nightclubs, call them what you like, but most of the former have a primary focus on drinks with a varying amount of food available.

Bar severs must be in tune to the needs of their customers. Are you in a sports bar, where people are watching a game on the television? Be sure to offer them any "team" specials.

Many bars have pool tournaments, dart competitions, and other various promotional theme nights. Granted the participants may be distracted and, in some cases, intensely focused on the challenge at hand; however, you must stay available and prepare to fulfill any needs that they may have. Don't assume that they don't want to be bothered. If they didn't want service, they would have their events elsewhere.

In dance clubs, where people tend to mingle, pay special attention to what people are wearing or note any aesthetic traits that stand out so that you can find them when you return from the bar.

If it's wing night at the pub, offer hot, spicy wings to encourage thirst. Interesting that alcohol stimulates hunger, and certain foods encourage thirst. Given that simple bonus, sales are a no-brainer even if you're in a bar that only serves appetizers.

2) **Appetizers:**

When it comes to selling appetizers, a great angle is to suggest and describe two different apps. Variety is the spice of life. Besides, customers' tastes and needs vary. And unless they've specified, you don't know if they have food allergies, specific dietary needs or preferences. Which two items should you mention?

There are different approaches to this question. Use whichever of the following methods suits your mood or that particular table.

- Recommend your personal favorite and a co-worker's favorite.
- Suggest a more expensive and a moderately priced item.
- Tell them which two are the most popular (biggest sellers).
- Mention one deep-fried and one healthier choice.
- Try one seafood and one chicken.
- Indicate an app. per person and one to share.

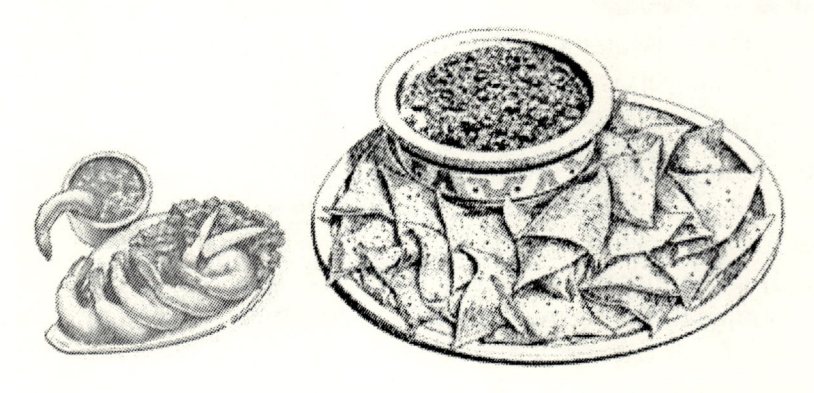

- Offer one finger food and one less messy.
- Pull two out of a hat if you must, but just do it. Offering two choices doubles your sale potential.

Plant a seed (suggestion) when taking first drink orders. "I'll leave you to browse the appetizer menu, while I get your drinks." Perhaps, take a simultaneous app. order.

Be sure to follow up when delivering their drinks. As you're placing the drinks on the table ask, "Have you decided which appetizer(s) you'd like?"

If they don't seem interested before or during their first or even second drink, don't give up, because alcohol stimulates appetite. Who knows, after a couple of cocktails, one or both of your two suggestions might not sound like such a bad idea.

3) Wine:

Since the right wine can enhance a meal, you would actually be doing your customers an injustice by not offering wine. Instead of simply saying, "Do you want some wine?" try "Can I assist you with the wine list?" (Nod/pause) "Do you prefer red or white?" (wait for a response) "Dry, medium or sweet?" (wait for a response) "In that case, may I recommend _____ or _____?"

Four excellent opportunities to suggest (sell) wine are:

i. Some customers order wine instinctively the moment they enter a restaurant, making your job easier.
ii. 59% of our surveyed customers prefer to hold off ordering wine until they order their entrée, often opting to start with cocktails. Therefore, when they order entrées, you should recommend an appropriate wine that will couple well with their dinner.
iii. Some are afraid you'll bring their wine too soon for their liking. That's okay, because the period between salad or soup and the entrée is the longest delay customers face, making it a perfect time to suggest wine again. "Your steaks will be ready in a couple minutes. We have a wonderful Cabernet Sauvignon that goes perfect with steak. Can I bring you a bottle (carafe or glass)?" (Nod)
iv. Then there are the underrated dessert wines. Many are surprised to find out how well, and which, wines will complement dessert items. See Chapter 11, *'Wining and Dining'* for suggestions on wines that go with desserts.

If your customers are debating as to whether or not they're in the mood for wine, offer to bring a sample of their choice. A one ounce sample can inspire or impress someone into a sale. Be sure not to pour samples to generously, or there'll be no need to order (or pay for) a glass.

Don't forget to up-sell!

If two or more customers order glasses of the same wine, suggest a bottle, carafe, or half carafe. It's more cost effective for them and more lucrative for the house and you.

FYI → Many carafes have a visible fill-line. Although a bartender will probably pour the wine, it is up to you, as the server, to ensure that it reaches the fill-line.

Don't instinctively bring the lower priced house wine, be sure they've seen the wine list and offer a medium and/or higher priced option.

How do you sell a second bottle of wine?

Finish pouring the first bottle. Hold up the empty bottle, and ask, Shall I bring you another bottle of Chardonnay now (Nod), or shall I wait to bring it with your entrées?" Say it casually (as if everybody has a second bottle) so they don't feel like they're overindulging any more than any other table.

4) **Sides**:

Customers are often too busy chatting or relaxing to think of accompaniments for their entrées. Some don't know that the menu offers various sides. Maybe they didn't read the entire menu. Others don't realize they want something until you plant a seed in their minds.

Some sides go traditionally well with certain entrées: steak with sautéed mushrooms, liver with onions, burgers with fries, pie with ice cream, etc. Other sides can be combined to make less traditional, but fabulous, couplings. It is our job to suggest these sides, traditional and untraditional alike.

Different establishments offer different sides, such as:

Salad	Cheese or Extra Cheese
soup (cup or bowl)	bacon
french fries	vegetables
baked potato	toast
rice	garlic bread
onion rings	sautéed mushrooms
battered veggies	sautéed onions
gravy	other sauces
à la mode	etc.

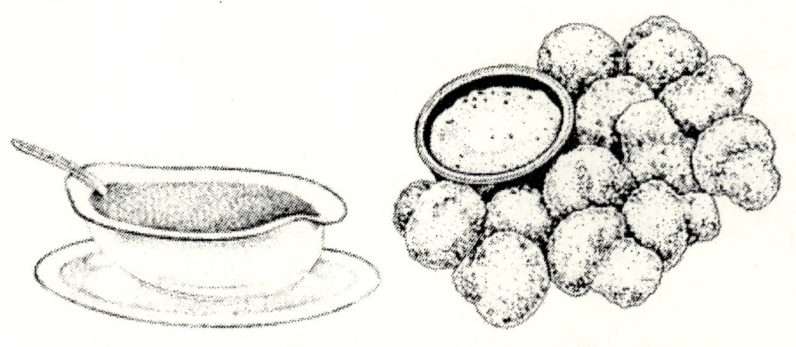

A dollar here, a couple dollars there, these little gems are quick, easy ways to please the customer, increase a bill, and raise your tip.

5) Drink refills:

Keeping glasses full is key to customer satisfaction and will assure a generous gratuity for you.

Helpful refill pitch hints:

- Instead of saying, "Would you like another drink?" try being more specific. "Would you like another screwdriver?" (Nod) Or simply, "Another screwdriver?" (Nod) Why are the latter better? Being specific makes the customers feel special because you remember what they were drinking. Also, the mere sound of their favorite drink is more enticing than a generic suggestion.
- If more than one person at the table is drinking, instead of asking just one person if they want "Another martini?" try "Another round?" And/or make a circular hand gesture. (Nod) Make eye contact around the table until you find someone who appears interested.

FYI → Important Fact: Studies prove that once customers have meals in front of them, the chances of them having another drink go down 93%. Given this knowledge, servers must offer more drinks before dinner is served.

Be sure to take care of those drinking soft drinks, as well. If you bring a round of drinks for the table, don't forget the designated driver. Don't play favorites; if the entire table is drinking soft drinks with free refills, the same goes; keep their glasses full and keep them satisfied. They are not insignificant simply because they aren't boozing it up. Plus, if the house does not offer free refills on soft drinks, there's another sale for you.

6) **Desserts:**

Any point after the entrées are ordered is a good time to recommend, "Be sure to save room for dessert," thus planting a seed in their minds.

When the time comes to pitch the actual sale, rather than saying "Do you want dessert?" try saying "Our home-made pecan pie is to die for, and the chocolate mousse is so light it melts in your mouth." (all the while nodding) Notice the two completely different choices. This concept works as well for desserts as it does for appetizers.

Giving an enticing, detailed description of a dessert can get mouths watering and customers ordering. Better still, if your restaurant has a dessert tray, cart or menu, use it. A picture is worth a thousand words and a sale.

The customer wavering between willpower and sweet surrender can be persuaded with some innovative suggestions.

➢ Offer to bring one dessert with two or more forks.
➢ Suggest desserts *to go* for a later indulgence.
➢ Offer cool desserts in warm weather (ice cream/sherbet) and warm desserts in cold weather (cobblers/warm apple pie [with cheese or à la mode]).

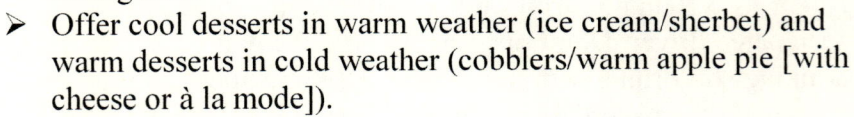

7) After-dinner drinks:

Before, after or simultaneously with your dessert sales pitch, offer after-dinner drinks: cognacs, brandies, liqueurs, dessert wines, ice wines, ports. If they have a brandy, a liqueur, or a cognac suggest a coffee to go with it. To many, coffee signifies the end of a meal; therefore, first tempt them with Grand Marnier, crème de menthe, Bailey's, etc.

Suggestive sales tip:

Let's say a customer isn't interested in any of the desserts listed on the menu, or they're thinking of having ice cream. Offer to drizzle a shot of their favorite liqueur over ice cream. Vanilla tastes great with almost anything. Some big favorites are green crème de menthe, butter ripple schnapps or Baileys. On chocolate, suggest banana liqueur or amaretto. On fruit flavored ice creams, suggest crème de cacao, Kalúha, or Tia Maria. And, by all means, experiment. Create your own. Use your imagination.

8) Coffees:

If they vote *no* to after-dinner drinks, recommend liqueur coffees (Spanish, B52, Irish) or a liqueur tea (Blueberry tea) or a liqueur hot chocolate. Always start with higher priced items, and then work your way down. After liqueur coffee, try cappuccino, espresso, mocha, latte, premium herbal teas, and finally, coffee, tea, or decaffeinated coffee.

Let's say a customer asks for a coffee before you get the chance to pitch liqueur coffees. In this case you can up-sell. "Would you like a liqueur on the side? Or "Would you like to try a Spanish coffee?" If they look at all interested, describe it to them using enticing adjectives. Many establishments have a 'House' coffee; be sure to take advantage of house hero products.

Personally, I sell the most liqueur coffees by asking my customers to 'build their own' by naming their favorite liqueurs or flavors. If they like almonds, Amaretto is perfect. Chocolate lovers will love crème de cacao. Oranges, Grand Marnier. Hazelnuts, Frangelico. And so on.

Rather than simply order-taking when someone asks for a tea, suggest a shot on the side or a liqueur tea. Blueberry Tea is the most popular liqueur tea (Grand Marnier, Amaretto, tea with an orange slice garnish. No sugar rim or whipping cream).

If the answer is no, recommend a premium tea (Earl Grey, Peppermint Breeze, English Breakfast, etc.). Go that extra step (if applicable) and offer to bring out the display box so that they may choose their favorite.

After having discussed eight add on/up-selling opportunities the following are other things to keep in mind and other ways to seal a sale:

- Customers are there to buy, not browse.
- Think of tips as commissions. The more you sell, the more tips you make.
- Studies show that customers are more likely to remember the first and last thing you say. Therefore, be sure to pitch an item at the beginning and end of your spiel. "Would you like a cocktail, wine, beer? Tonight's cocktail feature is our frozen daiquiri. We have lime, banana, strawberry and our new raspberry daiquiris." (Nod)
- Use props like menus, wine lists, table tents, special boards, etc. A guided tour of the menu or wine list will enable customers to make informed decisions. They'll thank you for it. As for table tents, when fully utilized they can actually do your job for you. Make a point of picking up the tent and pointing out cocktails and/or apps., then put the tent back on the table with those items facing the customer. After they've ordered drinks and/or apps., turn the tent to the specials. Once entrées are ordered, turn the tent to reveal desserts and/or specialty coffees. Let your props plant seeds for you.
- Feel free to actually point to the menu as you read details to the customer. This will help the customer focus on details and will also help you to learn the menu thoroughly.
- Use enticing adjectives when describing food and drinks: fresh, homemade, tender, juicy, seasoned, basted, mouth-watering, crisp, fruity, creamy, garden fresh, made to order, marinated, hearty, glazed, slow roasted, beer battered, smothered, popular.
- Whenever time permits, take the long way to a table with non-perishable goodies: cold appetizers, fancy drinks, desserts. Stroll by your other tables with such items carried at table eyelevel. And just watch those orders roll in.

- Watch for non-verbal indications that customers are interested in various items. Are they looking toward the bar to see what's on tap? Are they paying extra attention to the wine list? Do you notice them hovering on the appetizer section of the menu? Be sure to follow through on non-verbal interests.
- "The Nod." The Nod is the easiest, most effective way to get the sale. Instead of simply asking, "Sautéed mushrooms with your steak?" Make eye contact and nod while you're asking. This has been mentioned a number of times. All I can say now is try it. It works!

> Note: Being a great salesperson does not mean encouraging the customer who has already had several martinis and keeps trying to goose you and thinks they should be the designated driver to have another cocktail. We'll discuss these sorts of situations further in Chapter 21, 'Responsible Alcohol Service'.

Have you ever been in a restaurant and been disappointed because you:

- ❑ Forgot to order your favorite side dish?
- ❑ Had to wait an eternity for a drink refill?
- ❑ Noticed a fabulous sounding appetizer after ordering your entrée?
- ❑ Didn't get a chance to ask for a glass of wine until your meal was almost finished?
- ❑ Had a server who said you couldn't order extra this or extra that.
- ❑ Were never informed about specialty items?
- ❑ Didn't get offered dessert?
- ❑ Etc.

If so, the moral is obvious: stay sharp! Don't let your customers suffer these regrets. Seize every possible opportunity to Sell! Sell! Sell!

I read somewhere once that order takers are walking vending machines. I disagree. At least a vending machine *displays* its products. A brightly colored box of Smarties is a form of suggestive sales. An order taker doesn't even have that attribute.

> Nora, server of 9 years, is well known as one of the best salespeople in her restaurant. I'm not easily impressed, but Nora wowed me with a mathematical demonstration. She showed me how to make an extra $1000.00 per year through the use of simple suggestive sales. Sell five cocktails or appetizers at an average of $5.35 each per shift, multiply that by five shifts per week, times fifty weeks, and lastly by 15% gratuity. That's $1003.12. Just the fact that she was able to do the math without a calculator impressed me. The extra thousand in tips astounded me.
>
> $5.35 \times 5 \times 5 \times 50 \times 15\% = \$1003.12$

If you are still concerned about coming across as "pushy" keep two more things in mind. Firstly, the worst thing that can happen is they'll say no. Secondly, if they weren't prepared to spend a few dollars, they'd have stayed home and ate Kraft Dinner instead of going out to a place where everyone else is wining and dining.

SERVER'S NOTES

Chapter 11

Wining and Dining

You'll notice that the subject WINE is discussed often and at some length throughout this book. Why all the hoopla about fermented grapes? And what's in it for you?

- A glass, carafe or bottle of wine is a sale, which will boost the bill total and your tip.
- The correct wine can enhance the taste of a meal, just as the correct meal can enhance the taste of a wine, pleasing the customer and increasing your tip.
- A taste of the grape can set a mood or create an ambience, causing the customer to be more relaxed. Again, more tip for you.
- Wine, like other alcoholic beverages, stimulates appetite, encouraging customers to eat more, also bumping up the bill total and your tip.
- Customers are left feeling like they've been pampered, and they owe it all to you. One guess as to how they'll thank you.

So, if having wine with dinner is so commonplace, why is it that 65% of our polled servers don't know the first thing about wine? Fear of the unknown? Unaware of the importance? Don't understand wine lingo? Nobody ever taught them? Don't drink wine? Pure unadulterated laziness?

Regardless of your reason, this chapter will clear up some of the basics for you as quickly, concisely, and simplistically as possible.

Five "rules" about wine and food that you may have heard are:

1) Drink white wine with white meats like poultry and fish.

2) Drink red wines with red meat.

3) Wine doesn't go with salad.

4) Only sweet wines can be consumed with dessert.

5) And wine is for dining not for snacking.

Well, have I got news for you! Wrong! Wrong! Wrong! Wrong! Wrong!

Contrary to popular belief:

1) Certain fuller bodied white wines do go with red meat.

2) Some lighter bodied red wines do go with fish and poultry.

3) A wine with competitive acidity will actually enhance a salad, even one with an acidic dressing.

4) The right dry wines do go with dessert items.

5) And there are good couplings for wine and snack (junk) food.

There are many misconceptions shrouding the wide world of wine. A word to the wise is never to assume that certain couplings won't work. Be creative. Experiment.

Below is a list of surprising and not so surprising couplings.
- Pinot Grigio/Pinot Gris – salmon
- Sweet Sherry - a wide variety of desserts
- Sauternes - buttered popcorn, foie gras (goose liver), Roquefort cheese
- Cabernet Sauvignon - chocolate
- Red Burgundy - For fuller-styled red Burgundies, beef, beef bourguignon, game birds (such as duck or pheasant), rabbit, venison.
- Beaujolais - grilled chicken
- Pouilly-Fumé - goat cheese
- Vinho Verde - grilled fish
- Sauvignon Blanc - salad
- Italian Barbera - pizza
- Sancerre - goat cheese
- Barolo - braised beef
- Pinot Noir - salmon
- Muscadet - oysters
- Chablis - oysters
- Riesling - salad
- Red Bordeaux - lamb, venison
- Red Zinfandel - spicy nachos
- Gewürztraminer - foie gras (goose liver)
- Moscato d'Asti - breakfast (goes with whatever orange juice does)
- Port - walnuts, hazelnuts, and strong cheeses, such as Stilton, Gorgonzola, Roquefort, mature Cheddar, and aged Gouda

- Dry Sherry - almonds, green olives, shrimp or prawns, all kinds of seafood, soup
- White Zinfandel - hot dogs (mustard and sauerkraut)
- Red Burgundy (lighter bodied) - fish (especially salmon), seafood, chicken, turkey, or ham
- Amarone – Gorgonzola cheese

Taste is subjective. Feel free to use the aforementioned so-called "rules" as guidelines, but don't be afraid to experiment and discover some of your own intriguing couplings. For example, I am convinced that all wines (red, white, rosé, dry, medium, sweet, full-bodied, light bodied, you name it) taste great with all sweet/bell peppers (green, orange, purple, red, white, yellow).

For more wine and food pairings turn to the back of the book to the appendixes entitled, "Popular (Red/White) Wines Often Found in Restaurants and the Foods Which They Best Accompany."

FYI → Some Commonly Mispronounced Wines

	CORRECT	INCORRECT
Beaujolais	Boh-zhuh-lay	Boo-zhuh-lay
Moët	Moh-eht	Mo-way
Soave	Swah-veh	So-vay
Riesling	Reece-ling	Rize-ling/Reeze-ling
Rosé	Roh-zay	Rose
Montrachet	Mawn-rah-shay	Mont-rashay
Pinot Gris	Pee-noh gree	Pee-noh grease

Pronunciation, or fear of mispronunciation, can leave a server feeling intimidated by a wine. No one's saying you have to be able to speak a dozen different languages. Just make a point of learning your own wine list. Ask managers, wine reps, trainers, read books, surf the net, or visit a wine shop.

Although a basic glossary is located at the back of this book, below is a separate listing of some common wine terms and lingo.

Wine Glossary

acidity

Acids are a natural by-product of the growing and fermenting of grapes. Although all wine contains acid, acidity is more often associated with whites than with reds. A telltale sign of a highly acidic white is a pinching sensation on the sides of the tongue, a dry feeling in the mouth, and a tendency to salivate after swallowing. Positive words for describing wines with high acidity are crisp, snappy, tangy, vivacious. Positive words for describing less acidic wines are soft, smooth, mellow, delicate. Negative words *not* to be used regardless of a salesperson's individual opinion are bitter, sour, bland, tasteless.

aperitifs [ah-pehr-uh-TEEFs]

Dubbed by the French, a light alcoholic drink served before a meal to stimulate appetite. Popular aperitifs are champagne, dubonnet, sherry, lillet, and vermouth.

balance

>Well-balanced wines are wines that have a harmonious blend of alcohol, acidity, tannin, dryness, sweetness, fruit, oak, body, etc. When none of these components overpowers the others, a balance is achieved.

body

>The perception of weight, texture, or size of a wine in the mouth is referred to as body. Since words like weight and size tend to confuse, think of it this way, a small sip of a full-bodied wine can make your mouth feel full or weighed down. In the same turn, a large gulp of a light-bodied wine can leave little impression. Full-bodied wines go with full-flavored, hearty-textured, heavy foods. Light-bodied wines go with lighter tastes and textures. Still don't get it? Imagine a full-bodied wine with a mild filet of sole in a light cream sauce or a light-bodied wine with prime rib and strong horseradish. One would undoubtedly outweigh the taste of the other. For the layperson, many establishments carry a wide selection of medium-bodied wines. When coupling food and wine, body is more pertinent than color for balancing a diner's palate.

bouquet

>The smell or scent of a wine is a vital characteristic in the enjoyment of wine. Wines that have extremely pronounced and complex aromas are often described by their 'nose'.

brandy

From the Dutch "brandewijin" meaning "burned (distilled) wine" brandy is liquor which is aged in wood, contributing flavor and color. Although traditionally made from grapes, brandies can be made from other fruits such as apples, apricots, cherries, etc. In these cases the fruit is mentioned on the label (apricot brandy). By itself, the term brandy usually refers to a product made of grapes. The finest of all brandies is Cognac.

brut [BROOT]

A term usually applied to the driest (see dry) champagne and other sparkling wines. Brut wines are drier (contain less residual sugar) than those labeled "extra dry".

Champagne [sham-PAYN (Fr. Shah*m*-PAH-nyuh)]

True Champagne comes only from specific areas in France, from specific grape varieties, and is produced in a specific way. Since Champagne is a region in France, the French are dismayed that more and more winemakers are using the name Champagne on their labels. European Union regulations prohibit its members from using any form of the word Champagne (capitalized, abbreviated, or otherwise). In fact, if a label touts the royal word, and does not pass the criteria of the Champagne region, such wines are actually banned from sale in Europe. The quality of Champagne is often associated to the size of the bubbles. Smaller is better.

Cognac [KOHN-yak; KON-yak; Fr. Kaw-NYAK]

The finest of all brandies, Cognac, hails from the town of Cognac in western France. The term Fine Champagne on a cognac label indicates that 60% of the grapes come from Grande Champagne, which is the superior grape-growing section of Cognac. The words Grand Fine Champagne means all the grapes come from Grande Champagne. This double-distilled, oak-aged liquor comes in many distinctions: V.S. (very superior), V.S.O.P. (very, superior old pale), V.V.S.O.P. (very, very, superior old pale). The terms X.O., Extra, and Reserve indicate that a Cognac is the oldest put out by the producer.

corky/corked

When a wine has been negatively affected by a faulty cork, the term corky or corked is used. Moldy or musty smells and tastes indicate cork deterioration and in turn a corky wine. Experts estimate that 3 to 5 percent of wines suffer ruination because of bad corks. We won't go into every problem that can possibly occur with wine. This, however, needs mentioning, as it is the most common sign of a bad bottle.

dessert wine

Multitudes of sweet wines are referred to as dessert wines. As one would guess, if it tastes good with dessert, it's usually called a dessert wine. Several popular dessert wines are late harvest Riesling, port, sauternes, sherry, ice wine, and Auslese. They have higher sugar levels and higher alcohol levels. See *fortified wine* for more details.

dry

To say a wine is dry is to say that it is not sweet. A wine that is categorized as a zero (0) is a wine that has no sugar. So, logically, higher numbers indicate more residual sugar in a wine. To say that a wine is medium-dry means that it has a small amount of sugar (it's slightly sweet). The affects of tannin and acidity make dry wines seem dryer. Trocken [TRAWK-uhn] is German for dry. Sec is French for dry. And as previously mentioned, the term brut is used for champagne and sparkling wines.

earthy

A taste of the soil in which the grapes were grown, can be a bad thing if it is too pronounced and causes an imbalance in the overall impression of the wine. A slightly earthy undertone can also be a pleasant trait in the overall balance of a wine.

flinty

In certain dry white wines, especially Chablis, a slight metallic taste can be detected. Don't panic; if it is balanced with other aspects of the wine, this is fine.

fortified wine

The addition of brandy or a neutral spirit in order to elevate a wine's alcohol content is referred to as fortification. Generally having between 17 and 21 percent alcohol, some of the better known examples are port, sherry, Madeira, Malaga, and Marsala. In the United States, the legal term for all fortified wines is *dessert wines*. In Europe, fortified wines are called liqueur wines.

fruity/fruit

    Obviously, all of the wines we're talking about are made from fruit…grapes. But it's not that simple. A closer look reveals that the nose and the taste buds can, and often do, pick up characteristics reminiscent of other fruits such as apples, apricots, blackberries, blackcurrants, citrus fruits, peaches, pears, and raspberries to name only a few. Do not mistake this term to imply sweetness.

ice wine

    From the German "Eiswein" [ICE-vyn] meaning rich, flavorful *dessert wine*. Picking grapes that are frozen on the vine and then pressing them before they thaw makes Eiswein. Because much of the water in the grapes is frozen, the resulting juice is intensely concentrated. As many famous German wines, Eisweine are sweet, yet balanced by high acidity levels and are excellent for long-term ageing.

legs

    Legs will not enable a wine to get up and run away, but they show that a rich, full-bodied wine can stand up and announce itself. After a glass of wine is swirled, it often leaves the inside of the glass with a coating of tiny rivulets. These viscous rivulets vary in size and the time they take to return to the wine's surface. Unusually wide legs are often referred to as *sheets*.

mimosa

    A recommended mixture of two parts Champagne and one part orange juice, often served with breakfast or brunch.

oaky/oak

>Ageing wine in oak barrels or adding oak chips will bring forth a toasty, vanilla flavor and fragrance. Oaky flavors are quite popular, found more in reds, but also in whites, especially Chardonnays. Like all dimensions found in wine, too much of a good thing can be a bad thing.

oxidized

>Just like it sounds, a reaction of oxygen or air in wine results in deterioration. One telltale is a brown tinge in wines that are past their peaks. Although this is usually a bad thing, some oxidization can be helpful in softening young wines for early drinking.

port

>Typically served after a meal, ports are sweet, *fortified wines*, better know as *dessert wines*. The four basic categories are vintage, ruby, tawny, and white.

red wine

>You guessed it; red wine is made from dark-skinned grapes (red, purple, black, blue).

rosé/blush/pink wine

>These wines range in color from pale pink to apricot to salmon and also go by many other names, such as blanc de noir, Blanc de Pinot Noir, Cabernet Blanc, White Zinfandel, or Pinot Gris. Typically, in order to produce these rosé/pink/blush wines, red grapes are pressed, and then the skins are promptly removed to stop further

transfer of color. Another method of producing these lighter wines is by mixing red and white wines. Most are slightly sweet. Some are quite dry.

sake [SAH-kee; SAH-kay]

A contradiction to all we westerners know about the correlation between fruit and wine, nevertheless the U.S. Bureau of Alcohol, Tobacco, and Firearms categorizes this Japanese rice beverage in Class 6 -- wine from other agricultural products. Because it is made from grain (rice), some argue that sake should be classed as a beer. However, ranging from 12 to 16 percent, it is high for beer, low for a grain-based spirit, leaving it right in the range with most wines. Colorless or very pale yellow, sake is traditionally served warm in small porcelain cups called sakazuki. Although less heard of (especially in the west), Mirin is another popular Japanese rice wine.

sangria [san-GREE-uh]

From the Spanish for "bleeding" this blood-red beverage is a blend of red wine, fruit juices, soda water, fruit, and often liqueurs, and brandy or cognac over ice. When white wine is substituted, it is called sangria blanco (white sangria).

sherry

Although considered a *dessert wine*, sherry may be consumed before or after a meal. Ranging broadly in color, flavor, and sweetness, sherry is a multidimensional *fortified wine*.

sommelier [sum-mel-yay]

A specially trained wine expert who is responsible for putting a wine list together and for making sure that wines offered on the list complement the house's cuisine.

sparkling wine

Wines that contain bubbles of carbon dioxide gas (either produced naturally or added artificially) are considered sparkling wines. The term "crackling" wine is sometimes used synonymously with sparkling or, more frequently, in reference to wines only slightly bubbly compared to sparkling wines and even champagne.

spritzer [SPRIHT-ser]

Traditionally a blend of dry white wine and soda water over ice is referred to as a wine spritzer. Various twists on this use different kinds of wine (white, red, dry, sweet) and soft drinks (like ginger ale).

sweetness/sweet

Loosely translated, sweet wines are the opposite of dry wines, obviously because they contain more sugar. Sweetness can be noticed on the tip of the tongue the moment a wine enters the mouth.

tannin

Tannin is to a red wine what acidity is to a white. A main character factor found naturally in grape skins and seeds, tannin often dictates the personality of a red wine. Red grapes are fermented with the skins on, making reds higher in tannin than whites. A telltale sign of a highly tannic red is sudden drying of the mouth (especially between the cheeks and gums), a pinching sensation at the back of the tongue, and...have you ever taken a sip of strong, cold tea? Tannic wines give you that same sensation and often the same feeling of having sweaters on your teeth. Many people claim that they can't drink red wine because it gives them a headache; this is because of the high rate of people allergic to tannin. Try lighter bodied wines, with less tannin, if you sufferer from red wine headaches. Positive words for describing tannic wines are bold, firm, solid, hearty. Positive words for describing wines lacking in tannins are smooth, mellow, gentle, tame. Negative words *not* to be used regardless of a salesperson's individual opinion are harsh, overbearing, boring, flat.

white wine

Colorless, pale yellow, golden yellow, and amber wines are all considered white wines. Either made from light-skinned grapes (greenish, greenish yellow, golden yellow, pinkish yellow) or from dark-skinned grape juice that is immediately separated from skins, seeds, and pulp. The latter is the less used method.

All that said, you should be able to describe, suggest, and sell wine more easily and confidently.

But what about presenting, opening, and serving the wine? Don't feel alone if you need a crash course or refresher course on the basics. Many servers find wine service a discomforting, even intimidating, part of the job.

Five a, b, c instructions for presenting, opening, and pouring wine:

1. Presenting the bottle to the person who ordered the wine.

The point of this procedure is not mere pretension. It is so that the customer can check to make sure you brought the bottle they ordered and that the vintage is acceptable.

a) Hold the bottle at the base with one hand and at the neck with the other hand, with the label facing the customer who ordered the wine.

b) Allow them to investigate.

c) Upon their "okay" or nod, prepare to open the bottle.

2. The dreaded opening of the bottle.

Relax. Since you are equipped with your server's corkscrew, you need only the mechanical details.

What is a server's corkscrew?

It is the most compact, widely used corkscrew on the market (especially in restaurants, thus, the name, server's corkscrew). A straight, approximately three inch base holds three tools that fold into it, like a Swiss Army knife: a penknife, a small two inch curly thingamajig (we'll call it a drill), and a lever.

FYI → Most people are right-handed. Lefties may wish to take a reverse approach.

a) Keeping the bottle in your left hand (not resting on the table), use the small knife on your corkscrew. Grip the bottle with your left hand, and with your right hand, drag the flat, sharp side of the knife below the lip until the tip of the foil or shrink-wrapped sealer comes cleanly off. Be sure to cut *below* the lip to assure that the wine does not come in contact with the foil during pouring. [Always keep your knife blade sharp.] Discreetly tuck it into your pocket to free your hands for the next step (for safety purposes, fold the knife back into the base of the corkscrew before continuing). Although some bottles have an easy-open strip at the top of the bottle, you should use the knife for professional presentation.

b) With a firm grip still on the bottle, poke the point of the drill into the center of the cork, then guide (screw) the drill through the middle of the cork. Pressure need only be used for the first turn or two, as the drill will continue in naturally. Stop just short of penetrating the bottom of the cork. (Penetration often forces cork remnants into the wine.)

c) Next, place the lever on the lip of the bottle and push against the lever while lifting the cork up. Wiggle the cork out at the end, making as little noise as possible.

3. Presenting the cork for inspection.

a) Unscrew the cork from the corkscrew. Fold up your corkscrew and slide it into your pocket. The hardest part is now done.

b) Place the cork on the table...

c) Closest to the person who ordered the wine (beside their glass).

This gives them a chance to see if anything is wrong with the cork, indicating a potential problem with the wine. Truth be told, this stage is nearly always inconsequential. Most people who know about wine will not let any cork deter them from the true means of inspecting a wine: tasting it.

4. Allowing the customer to taste the wine.

a) Pour a small amount of wine (an ounce, a couple of mouthfuls, the point is...enough to taste/smell) in the glass of the person who ordered it.

b) Allow them to taste/smell it.

c) Wait for them to nod or mumble, "It's fine."

If, upon tasting the wine, a customer uses words like moldy, vinegary, chemical, or just plain weird, offer to take it back to the bar and bring them another bottle of the same. Or would they prefer a bottle of something else?

FYI → 74% of the surveyed servers with more than 10 years experience, have never had a bottle of wine returned because it was "bad".

When the wine is approved, you may begin pouring.

5. Pouring the wine.

a) Do not lift the wine glasses to meet the bottle. Leaving the glasses on the table, start with the person to the immediate left of the person who ordered the wine and begin pouring (a ladies first approach is a nice touch). In the case of a glass that is out of pouring reach or in an awkward location on the table, it is acceptable to move a glass, then pour (after the glass is back on the table). Do not touch the bottle to the glass. For red wine, fill the glass approximately halfway. For white, fill the glass approximately three-quarters full.

b) Continue pouring clockwise, serving the person who ordered last.

c) After each glass, twist your wrist, and the bottle, slightly as you raise it to avoid dripping on the table. At this point, you may (for the first time) place the bottle (label facing the customers) on the table.

Follow up: As their glasses get low, keep topping.

Remember not to fill the glasses too full.

And if they switch to a different wine, whether it is from white to red or from a lighter wine to a fuller, bring fresh glasses and start the process of presenting, pouring and opening from the beginning.

Opening wine takes practice, practice, practice. How or where, you may ask, can you get enough practice to become confident with the server's corkscrew?

- Offer to help the bartender open bottles.
- Practice at home. Enlist your family and friends as guinea pigs. In this case, you can practice the entire process from presentation and opening to pouring and tasting.
- Take your corkscrew to parties and offer to assist the host/hostess.

FYI → Step 2-b warns not to allow the drill to penetrate the bottom of the cork, as it will drive cork remnants into the wine. Conversely, if the drill is not inserted far enough, the cork may break. What do you do if this happens? If a cork breaks off and gets stuck in the neck of the bottle, reinsert the drill at a forty-five degree angle and repeat the above opening instructions.

> Gerard, server of 14 years, when serving wine, carries a linen napkin draped over his arm. After opening a bottle he wipes the lip, discretely slipping a napkin-wrapped finger into the bottle to ensure that no cork bits remain.

Based on server interviews, it has been brought to my attention that some restaurants are leaning toward uncorking wine at the bar. The admittedly inexperienced or lazier servers love the idea (less work for them). The stronger go-getters feel that this takes away from the dining experience, causing less opportunities for bumping up a tip.

FYI → 78% of our surveyed customers agree they wouldn't or don't appreciate having their wine opened at the bar. And 29% say they would or have refused to accept this procedure, insisting another bottle be brought, presented and opened at the table. The consensus was…if they wanted their wine pre-opened, they would have ordered a house wine or something with a screw cap.

Frequently Asked Questions...

What are proper serving temperatures?

Unless a customer requests otherwise, whites should be served chilled and reds shouldn't. We'll leave the exact temperatures to house policies. You may find it interesting to know: it was people living in drafty old castles who instated the old rule "Red wines should be served at room temperature". The cozy warmth that we consider room temperature is not what they had in mind for red wines. They were referring to 65°F or 18.3°C.

When and how should wine buckets be used?

Champagne is best kept very chilled. Although most people enjoy whites very chilled as well, some white wine lovers realize that over-chilling certain whites can dull their natural flavors.

Blush wines are most enjoyable when kept well chilled. It's not unheard of to submerge reds in a wine bucket for several minutes to bring them down to "old castle temperature".

To chill any wine, use a combination of ice and water, not just ice. Fill the bucket full enough to immerse the bottle so that all the wine is sufficiently surrounded.

What if a customer wants to let their red wine breathe?

Simply taking the cork out of a bottle will do very little to aerate a wine. Therefore, you may want to offer to decant the wine, which simply means, pour the wine into a decanter like a carafe with a wide neck. If they are satisfied with just having the bottle opened, then oblige their request.

Where do vintners come up with names for wines?

North American wines are more often named after their grape variety, while European wines are more often named after a region, town or wine maker.

Opening Champagne

No corkscrew necessary. In fact, using a corkscrew with champagne or sparkling wines could be dangerous. Owing to the carbonation, imagine the pressure behind that cork. Now imagine the cork and corkscrew flying across a dining room full of people. Not a pretty visualization, is it? It's all fun and games until somebody loses an eye. In fact, doctors have reported a regular increase of eye injuries on January first of each year. The increased consumption of Champagne on New Year's Eve is directly responsible for such wounds. Now, if you're one of those self-involved servers, who doesn't care about the people around you, keep in mind that over 80% of the injuries were inflicted on those opening the bottles. That would be you, if you're not careful.

Also, with regard to accidents, be sure the bottle hasn't been shaken, or it could spew everywhere when you open it. Even if the bottle hasn't been shaken, care must still be taken when opening bubbly wines. Most importantly, do not point the top of the bottle at anyone or anything breakable, just in case.

After removing the foil neatly, keep your hand or thumb over the wire cage when untwisting it, then remove the cage carefully.

To avoid breaking the cork, twist the bottle off the cork rather than the cork off the bottle. As you twist, keep a balance of inward pressure on the cork to *ease* the cork out. If it helps, brace the base of the bottle against your hipbone.

Let's discuss the popping issue. When opening wine in a restaurant, we must remember that we are, indeed, in a restaurant, not in a locker room or at the christening of a ship. For caution from injury or damage, for care in not wasting the precious liquid, for class and style, silence is golden in the case of serving champagne. After all, the reason that Champagne and other sparkling wines are special is their bubbles. The complex process of carbonation is more costly and creates the unique character in each wine. To recklessly liberate the bubbles would be a disservice to the consumer.

The most crucial moment is when you hear the gas begin to escape around the edges of the cork. The goal here is to let the gas hiss out slowly without allowing the cork to escape your grasp. The pop that follows should be barely audible, indicating that you have done your job properly. Wine will not spew out of the bottle and the bubbles will not be released by an outburst of foam.

Although you should not typically remove glasses from the table when pouring, it is acceptable with sparkling wine to tilt the glass to avoid an overabundance of foam. As with other wines, you should never fill a glass to the top. Champagne glasses should be poured approximately to the three-quarter level.

Hopefully, this chapter has dispelled some myths, answered some questions, and eased some minds. If you're still thinking, "Do I really have to know that much about wine?" or "Is wine really that important?" read the following:

Several years ago, I read a fantastic book entitled *"Fear of Wine an introductory guide to the grape" text by Leslie Brenner/illustrated by Lettie Teague.* I applaud the comments on page 250 about tipping. Check out this excerpt addressed to wining diners, *"...be sure to reward good wine service in your* *gratuity. A server often has to go out of his or her way to know the wines, and this should be reflected in the tip. We all know that good service should be rewarded with a tip of 15 to 20 percent of the total bill before taxes. But many people are stumped when they have to figure out tipping when dinner included an expensive bottle of wine. Current etiquette requires that you calculate the tip on the entire bill, including the wine."*[1]*

Thank you, Leslie! So few books address the etiquette of tipping. I agree with almost everything quoted. The only point where my thinking differs is the part where tipping is done on the total of the bill "before taxes".

The way I see it, most restaurants or servers have a policy about "tipping out" or sharing tips with their support staff (bussers, bartenders, hostesses, etc.). The amount which is passed on or shared varies greatly, most often based on a percentage of the servers' sales -- including taxes. Point being, since the server is tipping on the taxes, why shouldn't the customer?

Aaanyway, aside from my little commentary, I hope the quote about wine and tips made this information worthwhile.

As a wannabe sommelier, I could go on and on, which you're probably thinking I have. So let me end this chapter by saying, don't whine that you don't know about wine. Learn, ask, read, look it up, pay attention, sample. If the boss offers an opportunity to sample, go for it (provided you wouldn't be better suited for a twelve-step program). Wine tasting can be informative and yummy.

A server who is informed about wine and the wine menu will not only appreciate the importance of wine with a meal, but will also dazzle the customer.

---

*[1] Fear of Wine; Bantam Books/November, 1995. All rights reserved. Text copyright ©1995 by Leslie Brenner Library of Congress ISBN 0-533-37464-8. Published simultaneously in the United States and Canada.

SERVER'S NOTES

PART THREE

FINE TUNING

In This Part

Chapter 12: Above and Beyond - Dazzling the Customer

Chapter 13: Table Maintenance

Chapter 14: Prioritize and Organize

Chapter 15: Scan and Plan

Chapter 16: Read Your Tables

SERVER'S NOTES

Chapter 12

Above and Beyond - Dazzling the Customer

What do customers want from you?

The best way to answer this conundrum is to ask yourself the same question. What do you want when you're the customer? If you're like most customers, you want all the things discussed in this book (positive, efficient, courteous, informative, prompt service). Moreover, you probably want what you want when you want it. Is that too much to ask? No! That's a server's job.

How can you go above and beyond the call of duty?

How can you go above and beyond a customer's expectations?

Every server has their own style, but below are a few suggestions to give you the general idea.

➤ Upon first contact with your customers, introduce yourself. By telling them your name, you're making yourself human in their eyes, instead of a piece of restaurant furniture.

- If welcomed, customer interaction is a significant aspect of service, further assisting in making them feel at home and comfortable.
- Productivity must take priority over socializing. Show them you know what you're doing, and dazzle them with your ability to combine professionalism with friendliness.
- Inform your customers about cook times. "Your appetizers will be ready in about ten minutes." If they have plans after dinner, they'll appreciate your concern for timing. If they're simply debating which wine/drink will go well with their apps., they'll appreciate the update. If they don't care either way, hey, no harm no foul.
- Do not refill coffee cups to the rim; leave room for cream, sugar and stirring.
- If you know they like their coffee black, fill'er up. It will be appreciated because most people who drink black coffee tend to drink lots of it.
- Don't play shy. Let them know you're there and you're serving them. Servers who keep their profile too low could be risking keeping their tips low as well.
- Pay attention. Be observant, attentive. Instead of saying, "Would you like another beer?" try "Another Coors Light?" Were you nodding when you read that? If not, read it again with a nod and an inquisitive, yet confident, tone in your voice. Paying attention to details like a beer brand demonstrates not only great sales technique, but also it is impressive that you care enough to note details.
- Offer suggestions and input. Inform them which menu items are most popular. Be prepared to answer questions. If you know your stuff and want to sell, sell, sell this will be no problem.
- For your customers with ribs, wings, or other finger foods,

pamper them with a finger bowl. Fill a small bowl halfway with lukewarm water and a slice or wedge of lemon, and place it on a small plate with extra serviettes or a linen napkin.

➤ Bring a side plate for meals that have bones or shells.

➤ Does your establishment have pepper mills? If so, don't neglect to offer fresh ground pepper with the appropriate dishes. Five or six turns should be sufficient. To adjust the size of the grind, turn the knob or bolt at the top of the peppermill. If the customer comments that they can't see the pepper, grind once over the empty, white surface of the plate to show that it is working.

➤ Be attentive to special needs such as: allergies, diets, preferences. For example, vegetarians will want to know that there are no animal products or by-products (like cooking oil) used in the recipes or preparation of their food.

➤ My publisher travels with her diabetic Mom, and says, "The server who knows some broad nutritional information can be quite helpful -- as well as one who knows to bring bread or crackers to the table in case the meal is running late. Since diabetics need to eat on time, this is appreciated. The same should be done for anyone taking medication that requires food"; pay attention to see if they have pills or are looking in a pocket or purse for medication.

➤ If there are any problems with food or drinks, handle them promptly and effectively. Apologize, replace the item in question and inform a manager where house policy dictates.

➤ If a customer makes an out-of-the-ordinary request, you should do your best to accommodate. Let's say that a customer wants to order an item that has been taken off the menu; perhaps the kitchen still has the necessary items to facilitate that special request. But be sure to check with a manager before tampering with standard policy.

> Be clear and concise when talking to your customers.

> Fran, server of two and a half years, openly admitted that she talks fast when she's busy. One day, she asked a man if he wanted soup or salad with his meal. The man, obviously intrigued, asked, "What's in the super-salad?"

> Give everyone the same non-judgmental service. Just because they aren't spending big money today, doesn't mean they won't be back another day with larger appetites, more money to spend, and perhaps several friends.

> Thanking customers by name, if possible, will help build or maintain rapport for future visits. When they are pleased with your service and attentive demeanor, it is likely that you'll be seeing them again. Perhaps, your customers will become regulars. And what better way to greet your regulars than by name. How? They may introduce themselves. You could check the reservation book. Or simply look at their credit card when they pay.

> Keep in mind that a customer is a customer. Be kind to everyone with whom you interact. Your co-worker's customer today may be yours tomorrow. If someone else's customer asks you for something and you blow them off because they're not in your section, you can bet your bottom dollar they'll remember you and your indifference the next time they come in and sit in your section.

These are only a few examples of service above and beyond the call of duty. Use your imagination. Be creative.

If you should sadly notice a distinct, long-term decrease in tips, you shouldn't blame the customers until you first look to yourself.

Earlier, the question was posed, if you're a vegetarian, who cringes at the sight of red meat, are you going to be able to pull off the role of a steakhouse server? I'd like to add, if you are going to chameleonize yourself, do it right. You shouldn't have to lie *much*, but you may have to keep some things to yourself. Picture it, you work at a high volume seafood eatery, and you're allergic to shellfish. The customer asks, "How's the seafood linguini?" You answer, "Beats me. I can't eat the stuff, or I break out and balloon up like a speckled blowfish." I think not! Instead, how about saying, "The seafood linguini is our most popular pasta dish." Or better yet, show them the dish with words. "The seafood linguini is tiger shrimp, sea scallops, tender crab meat, and Portobello mushrooms sautéed with garlic butter, served over a bed of tender linguini noodles in a light lemon-herb sauce."

You owe it to your tips to dazzle your customers. Moreover, you owe it to the paying customers. Lest we forget, they can eat at home. It is that something extra you provide that draws them away from their tables and attracts them to yours.

And when customers come to your tables, they often bring the entire family with them. That means adults and children!

Sugar and spice, snakes and snails, children can be adorable, sweet, little charmers; or they can be uncivilized hellions.

Serving children can be a nightmare, but it is a reality that we must make the best of. The children are likely not tipping, and their parents might not tip either if they notice their server demonstrating a lack of patience or pleasantness.

- Feel free to comment how cute a child is or how adorable a baby is or even ask a child how they are today. Be careful. Be polite, but don't fuss too much or else the child/children will be distracted by you and won't eat their meals.

- To keep a fast pace, try seating children facing a wall so that they won't be distracted by the goings on in the restaurant.
- Some advise that we take food and drink orders from parents, not children; while others insist on the opposite. This is where servers have to use their people skills to interpret the best approach. A good idea is to address the children directly and hope that the parents will interject if they prefer.
- Offer to bring kids' meals A.S.A.P.
- Offer to hold kids' drinks until mealtime.
- As much as we dread parents who allow their children to run around wildly, be alert, avoid bumps, spills and burns.
- Especially where children are concerned, caution must be taken with hot plates. Re-plating onto cooler plates when necessary is considerate and safer.
- Don't fill drinks too full.
- Don't serve anything that you wouldn't want served to you. Wipe the rims of plates, Ask the cook (nicely) to correct any unappealing dishes.
- To avoid messes in advance, casually move sugar bowls, salt and pepper shakers from reach of little hands.
- Offer high chairs, tucking the chair as close as comfortably possible to the table, thus reducing spillage on floors.
- Have extra napkins on hand for sticky fingers and spills.

Although we must put extra work into keeping tables with children clean and clear, all tables must be kept comfortably tidy. If you want to keep your customers happy, table maintenance should always be high on your list of priorities.

Chapter 13

Table Maintenance

Table maintenance refers to the acts of refilling and topping up drinks and the removal of all unnecessary items from the table. Maintain service at all times, maintain sales standards, maintain customer comfort, maintain cleanliness.

Offer refills on bar drinks as well as soft drinks. Let them know whether the refills are free; they'll appreciate the information. And top up coffee cups, water glasses and wine glasses where applicable.

What about keeping tables free of clutter? The comfort of your customers is in your hands. Who can relax when the table is cluttered with items that are no longer of use?

Table maintenance need not be seen as a bother to you or the customers. It can be done while you're at the table for other reasons. When you're delivering a second drink, you can take away the first empty glass. Or upon presenting wine, you can take away salad, soup or appetizer dishes.

Other benefits of table maintenance are that it gives you a chance to discreetly monitor their progress, see if they need anything at that moment, top their wine glasses, schmooze with them.

> Elaine, server of 6 years and a self-professed snoop, says she gets some of her best dirty jokes from eavesdropping while she tidies her tables.

Regarding table maintenance, what are some of the most commonly neglected items?

- Glasses.

  From aperitifs and cocktails to wine and after-dinner drinks, glasses take up a lot of table space. Besides, taking one glass away gives you an opportunity to offer a round of refills.

- Bottles.

  Whether it's a beer bottle, water bottle, or wine bottle, it should be taken away the moment it is empty. Don't forget to offer a refill.

- Side/bread and butter plates.

  If it's no longer functional, take it away. Side plates or bread and butter plates somehow seem to be the most neglected. When and how bread is served may change the optimal time to remove these. If you can't decide sooner, with the entrée plates is usually safe. When in doubt, ask the customer, "Are you finished with this plate?" or "May I take this for you?"

- Bread baskets or breadboards.

  These can take up a lot of table space and, therefore, must also be removed when they are no longer needed.

- Cutlery.

  Used or unneeded utensils should be removed. Clearly, a butter knife is not needed to drink coffee, and a soupspoon is not needed to eat dessert.

- Ashtrays.

  The majority (82%) of the interviewed servers agrees that ashtrays should be changed when they have no more than 2-3 butts in them. The reason little has been said about ashtrays is simply because laws are prohibiting smoking in public. If your establishment is an exception that still allows smoking, it is extremely important to change ashtrays, especially just before food is delivered to a table.

- Condiments.

  Sauces, jellies, jams, ketchup, vinegar, butter, salad dressing, steak sauce, hot sauce, etc., when customers are finished with such items (not before), remove them from the table.

- Garbage.

  From rib bones, empty sugar packets, and empty creamers, to straws, unwanted garnishes, and candy wrappers, garbage has no place on a properly maintained table.

- Crumbs.

  Using a crumber (scraper), crumb brush or napkin, wipe crumbs off tables onto a small plate (not a hand or the floor).

- Dessert plates.

  Another often neglected item: if you can remember to go to a table to give your customers their bill, and you can remember to go back to collect their payment, why on earth wouldn't you take their dessert plates away?

  By the time you, or a busser, are ready to clean a table, the only things that should be left to clear are coffee cups, spoons and maybe water glasses.

  You should keep your tables maintained for your customers' comfort. However, if you don't do it for the customers, do it for yourself, for the tips, and to help keep you more organized.

SERVER'S NOTES

Chapter 14

Prioritize and Organize

At any given moment, there are umpteen duties that need your attention. Your first task is to prioritize and organize those duties. A combination of elementary factors must be blended and sorted so that you may address your responsibilities based on priority and with optimal organization. Shall we take a course in elementary basics?

- Geography

Which chores are closest to you, to the bar, to the kitchen, to the servers' station and to each other? Can you multitask?

- Mathematics

Say you have a table of ten who need their plates cleared and a deuce who need cola refills. If you only have forty-five seconds before the dinners for a third table are up, your time restraints obviously send you to the deuce first.

- Chronology

Who asked for something first? Who's been waiting longer?

- History

Who are your regular customers, and what do they usually want, need or expect? If you know certain regulars always have coffee immediately after they finish their entrées, you can save steps by bringing coffee with you on the way to clear their plates.

- Protocol

Such subjects are not taught in our modern-day schools, still many things can be said about etiquette; in this case we'll focus on one of the oldest rules: ladies first. 82% of the surveyed customers said to forget about sexism where the ladies first rule comes into play. Very few will be offended if you serve ladies first, where many will take offence if you do not.

- Genealogy

Serve ladies first, and if there is more than one lady at the table, serve the older of the ladies first. Another special situation that lands in this subsection is wedding service. The bride is always first, followed by the groom, then the female attendants and the groomsmen. After serving the wedding party, head for the parents and grandparents of the bride and groom, then the rest of the family in order of their closeness to the happy couple and finally friends.

- Literature

Take proper notes. It's not necessary to write a novella for every table. Simply write orders neatly and thoroughly to avoid errors

- Business

Sell. Up-sell. Make recommendations.

- Law

The customer is always right.

- Sociology

Chatting it up with co-workers is not out of the question. Just remember that co-workers aren't going to tip you. When you have tables, your customers must be your top priority.

What, you may ask, are some issues or situations that take top priority?

- Greet newly seated tables quickly. Worst case scenario, say "I'll be right with you." Finish what you're doing and return promptly.
- Problems with food or drinks are a priority. Handle it before it becomes a serious problem.
- If some guy needs his third coffee refill and there are delicate pasta dishes waiting under an unforgiving heat lamp, take the food. Buddy's cup isn't going anywhere.
- Quality checks. After meals are delivered, no more than two or three minutes should pass before you do a quality check, which simply means checking to see if their food is satisfactory. Is it cooked properly? Is it hot enough? Does it taste good? The sooner you do a quality check, the sooner you can correct any problems and/or move on to other chores.
- Side-work is necessary, but the customer always comes first.
- Keep service stations and work areas stocked and organized. Clean as you go and messes are less likely to pile up.

By staying a step ahead, while always thinking of doing these maintenance activities, you will always be ready for a rush.

A broad attention span will keep your section flowing smoothly and your tips flowing in.

SERVER'S NOTES

Chapter 15

Scan and Plan

You look both ways before crossing the street so that the hazards of the road don't plough you down. So why aren't you using your peripheral vision at work to avoid hazards like the weeds and getting stiffed?

42% of the interviewed servers admit (at least occasionally) to the bad habit of either locking their eyes straight ahead to their destination or gawking downward as if they're counting the floor tiles. Locking and gawking are two sure fired ways to leave you oblivious to what's happening around you. Scanning and planning, on the other hand, are the ways to keep you aware and efficient.

As you're passing through your section, visually scan each table. And, if you're not busy, stand apart from the section and start scanning and planning to keep you from getting in over your head.

In Over Your Head?

Ask the what, which, when, why, where, who, and hows.

? At what stage of dining are my customers currently involved? What do they need now?
? Which of my tables have just been seated? Which of my tables needs to be cleaned or is currently being cleaned by a busser?
? When did that table receive their meals? Is it time to do a table

check? Clear plates? Offer dessert? Etc.
? Why is that table giving me the eye? Do they need something?
? Where are potential problems with food or drink?
? Who needs more water, coffee, pop, serviettes, etc.?
? How can I make my customers' dining experience more pleasurable?

Scan and plan. Scan and plan.

If you've made it through all of these questions without finding anything that needs doing, then ask the what, which, when, why, where, who, and hows again.

? What stage are my tables approaching? What will they need then?
? Which of them is a priority?
? When did I order that table's food?
? Why isn't their food ready yet? Is there a problem in the kitchen? Should I bring this to the attention of a manager?
? Where can I make another sale?
? Who is ready for the bill? Who is ready to pay?
? How can I bump up my tip?

Scan and plan. Scan and plan. You can't do this enough.

FYI → Keeping a close eye on your section also reduces the chances of D & Ds. Read your tables and stay on top of things.

Chapter 16

Read Your Tables

If this expression sounds like it's referring to mind reading, in a way, it is. Feel out your customers (figuratively, of course). Be aware of the different moods of each table.

Are they out for a romantic dinner (holding hands, sitting on the same side of the table or flirting)?

Are they stopping in for an after-funeral dinner (all wearing black, somber, or red-eyed from crying)?

Or is it a happy occasion, a birthday, anniversary, graduation dinner? Do you see balloons? Gifts? Cards?

Are they dressed in formal wear like prom dresses? Or are they still wearing their matching bowling shirts?

Pay attention to body language. Are they making a lot of eye contact with you? Joking around? Inviting you into their conversations? Or are they whispering? Discussing business? Speaking to you only when necessary?

Are they checking their watches often? Have you heard them mention show times? Or are they in no rush to order? Relaxing over cocktails or bottles of wine?

Have you checked the reservation book to see if any occasions are listed?

The previous questions will tell you how much personality and panache to apply.

After having touched on all of these signals, caution must be taken to read, but not to pre-judge. Don't make the mistake of misreading or categorizing people or groups of people. Although certain types of people have been assumed to be poor tippers, you can't judge a book by its cover.

- Students

Granted, students are usually on budgets, but don't forget how a lot of them make ends meet: serving. And who tips better than a person who works for tips?

- Seniors

If you can't be good to them out of basic respect for your elders, then do it because their money is as good as the next guy's. And just because they want to know if you have a senior's discount doesn't mean they won't tip you.

> Evelyn and Ron M. are an eighty-year-old couple and just happen to be frequent diners. The unsuspecting eye would never peg them as big tippers. However, thanks to years of waitressing, their daughter was able to support herself through law school. Now they spend the winters in their daughter, the lawyer/ex-waitress's, timeshare in Florida.

- Women

This is, after all, the twenty-first century! With more and more women in the workforce, women often have as much money as men do. And, whatever you do, don't blow off your female customers because you assume the man is paying, or you could get a rude awakening.

- Certain nationalities

What can I say here, except tsk, tsk, tsk!

- Casually or shabbily dressed

Don't judge a book by its cover. Even the most elite patrons like to wear sweats from time to time.

- People who aren't spending much

Maybe they aren't spending the wad this time, but what about the next time?

Sure, the aforementioned stereotypes are occasionally true, but to assume the worst is to risk a potential tip.

Back to the topic at hand, reading your tables. Not to discourage you, but sometimes despite your best efforts to read your tables without making snap judgments, you'll still have complaints.

SERVER'S NOTES

PART FOUR

The Heat Is On

In This Part

Chapter 17: Dealing With Complaints

Chapter 18: Don'ts

Chapter 19: Safe Serving

Chapter 20: S#*~ Happens

Chapter 21: Responsible Alcohol Service

SERVER'S NOTES

Chapter 17

Dealing With Complaints

Although you do your best, you will occasionally get complaints from your customers. How you handle the dilemma can be the difference between a happy, tipping customer and a lost customer along with future gratuities.

Customers may complain if:

- Food is undercooked.
- Food is overcooked.
- Quality of food or drinks is questionable.
- A customer gets the wrong food.
- Service is unsatisfactory.
- A staff member spilled something on the customer.
- Food takes too long.
- Entrees come too soon, while customers are still eating salad, for instance.
- After ordering, the customer is informed that something they wanted has been 86ed.
- A foreign object is found in food or drink.
- The list here could go on and on; however, let's focus on a more *helpful* list that tells how to handle complaints.

If a complaint arises:

- Find out why. Listen carefully and attentively.
- Repeat the complaint back to the customer to ensure that you understand fully.
- Apologize appropriately.
- Acknowledge the customer's feelings (anger, disappointment, frustration, etc.).
- Alert a manager immediately.

Never:

- Let a customer leave feeling you do not care.
- Argue with a customer.
- Criticize customers or other employees.
- Ignore problems.
- Challenge a customer.
- Make excuses.

All that said, some customers will be just plain difficult. How do you deal with difficult customers?

If only there was a simple solution to this dilemma. Remember what Mom said about catching more flies with honey than you do with vinegar? She also says, "Kill them with kindness." Even the nastiest, most irrational customer will have a hard time lashing out at you if you stay calm and polite at all cost.

Don't keep a potentially difficult customer waiting for anything.

Even if everything is going perfectly, the customer shouldn't have to *wait*. You're the *wait*er/*wait*ress.

Perhaps, the best advice anyone could give is...keep a manager abreast of any potentially volatile situation. If all your attempts fail, ask a manager to deal with the predicament. One of the responsibilities of management is to maintain public relations and customer satisfaction.

Even if it hurts, remember the old rule "the customer is always right".

Lastly, don't let the few bad apples you come across ruin your day or, worse yet, your attitude toward your other tables. Let's face it, you're already the lowest paid employee on the planet. Don't compound that by blowing your chances to make tips.

SERVER'S NOTES

Chapter 18

Don'ts

Now that we've gone over what to do, it's time to learn some more basics about what NOT to do.

> **Goofy Don't Tip:**
>
> Don't eat yellow snow.

- 👎 Don't chew gum. Unless you're working at a theme restaurant, like a Mel's Diner (kiss my grits) spoof, for goodness sake, spit out that chewing gum. It's unprofessional, unacceptable, and looks horrible.
- 👎 Don't nibble while you're on duty. If a customer sees you chewing, they'll wonder if you pilfered food off of their plate.
- 👎 Don't wipe your hands on your apron or clothing.
- 👎 Don't stand with your arms crossed. If you know anything about body language, you'll know that those arms folded across your chest send out a message that says you're closed minded and unapproachable, to say the least.
- 👎 Don't stand with your hands on your hips. What was just said about body language also applies to this unprofessional stance. Aside from the visual connotations, bony elbows are formidable weapons to those around you. Other servers and customers shouldn't have to maneuver their way around your expanded wings. If you can't flap them and take flight, pull those elbows in.
- 👎 It's already been said, "Keep Busy". But if you still insist on

standing around, or if you have to pause to arrange your priorities, stay out of the way. If someone else is hard at work (making more tips than you), don't be the obstacle that stands between them and their objectives: coffee, kitchen, bar, etc.
- Don't pick up a glass by the rim. Don't put down a glass by the rim. Don't touch or handle a glass anywhere near the rim. Always handle glassware by the lower portion of the glass (the stem where applicable). Although the spider grip (inserting fingers inside the rims of dirty glasses, cups, or bottles,) is effective when clearing tables, it is unsanitary. Would you put your hand in five different people's mouths and then serve another customer's food with that same hand?
- The Same goes for cutlery. Don't touch the *eating end* of utensils.
- Don't run your fingers through your hair, rub your eyes, scratch, chew your nails, etc. Nobody wants to see your hand on your nose or derrière and then carrying their food.
- If you use pepper mills, don't carry them under your arm. It's disgusting. No one wants 'fresh ground armpit' on their food.
- Don't ever say, "Sorry, that's not my section." The reason for repeating and repeating this no-no is because it's one of our most mentioned customers' top ten pet peeves. (see the appendix at the back of the book for the other nine.)
- Don't let your customers 'run' you. If one person orders a drink or needs something from the kitchen, make sure to check with the rest of the table to make sure they're all fine.
- Don't whine and moan that you hate your job, hate your customers, wish you were somewhere else, hope you can get off early, etc. Not only is this attitude bad for morale, it will also shine through to your customers and hurt your tips.

Goofy Don't Tip:

Don't cook bacon in the nude.

Chapter 19

Safe Serving

We're not talking about wearing a condom on the job. We're talking about physical safety and health precautions.

Physical safety

➤ To reduce risk of back injuries, bend at the knees when you pick up heavy items.

➤ Tread carefully in the dish-pit. Even the cleanest, most organized dish-pit can be slippery.

➤ Always clean up spills or sweep up messes to prevent accidents. From dropped butter pats to weather dragged in on shoes or boots, pay special attention to floors.

➤ New shoes can be slippery. Experienced servers recommend scuffing the bottoms. No one is suggesting that you wreck your new shoes. For the record, scuff the *bottoms*, as in soles, of the shoes. No, you don't have to buy a mythical shoe scuffer. Just find some coarse pavement (the parking lot at the mall, the sidewalk in front of the restaurant), and drag your feet a few times. Guaranteed to reduce slippage.

➢ Be sure that shoelaces are not too long and are securely tied to avoid tripping.

➢ Warn customers of hot plates, before you place meals on the table. Metal, cast iron or casserole dishes that have been in a scorching hot oven are often used for presentation or practicality, which means they won't be re-plated or cooled down before reaching the customer. So be sure to carry them accordingly and warn customers appropriately.

➢ Always use an ice scoop to put ice in a glass. Using your hands to scoop ice is unsanitary, and dipping a glass into an ice machine, ice sink, or ice bucket is everything from dangerous to inconvenient. If a glass breaks in the ice, and you see it, you'll have to empty the ice and clean out the receptacle to ensure all remnants of glass are gone. Worse yet, if a glass breaks or chips and you do not see it, someone could be seriously injured.

Health precautions

Rotate and restock condiments, juices, dairy products, and any other perishable foods or beverages. Check expiration dates where applicable.

Never store any products in cans after opening (tomato juice, for instance, is dangerous when stored in an opened can). You should always transfer canned products into glass or plastic containers after opening.

⚠ Raw foods must never come in contact with cooked foods.

⚠ Be sure chemicals are used and stored appropriately. Most toxic chemicals have warning labels stating things like store in a cool, dry place, avoid contact with skin, keep away from heat or flame, seek immediate medical attention if...etc., etc., etc. You get the idea. Bottom line, carefully read and follow all label recommendations.

⚠ You should never work when you're ill since this could mean that germs are spread not only from you to other employees and customers, but also to the food and beverages that you will be handling. Sick employees are better suited for sipping chicken broth rather than serving it.

⚠ Whether sick or healthy, all employees who handle food should wash their hands regularly, especially after coughing, sneezing, scratching, smoking, or handling cash or chemicals.

Lastly, remember when working with the public for a living, all the health and safety precautions in the world can't stop s#*~ from happening.

SERVER'S NOTES

Chapter 20

S#*~ Happens

No matter how prepared you are, how efficient you are, how careful you are, how polite you are, sometimes s#*~ happens. Things could go sour if:

- You write down an order wrong.
- A customer slips or trips.
- You drop or break something.
- Customers are angry because the hosting staff lost their reservation.
- Two servers collide and drop a tray of food.
- You deliver table 3's food to table 13.
- Heaven forbid, a customer finds a foreign object (like a hair) in their food.
- You ring something in under the wrong table.
- Someone short-changes you.
- You spill something on a customer.
- A customer cuts their lip on a chipped glass.
- Etc.

There are some circumstances where nothing can be done to stop s#*~ from happening. When it's too late for prevention, redemption is the next step to extinguish a bad situation. Whether dealing with a serious blunder or a minor faux pas:

➢ Remain calm.

➢ Quickly analyze the situation.

➢ Apologize appropriately (be sincere).

➢ Do what you can to make amends i.e. offer to have the house pay for dry cleaning, clean up messes quickly, offer to promptly replace mistakes with correct orders, call 911. Whatever the situation, speed is crucial.

➢ Inform a manager if necessary. In case you haven't noticed, the surveyed servers and I are firm believers in letting management handle the frowns, while we handle the smiles and the tips. The surveyed servers agree that it's best to be as polite and helpful as possible and then disassociate one's self from negative situations.

Kendra, server of fifteen years told me a horrifying story about the worst thing that ever happened to her. It went something like this: she spilled nearly a half a pot of steaming hot coffee on a customer's leg. Kendra tore a tablecloth from the nearest table, shattering every dish that was dragged off with her one foul sweep (she's no quick-handed magician). Dropping to her knees, she began patting and wrapping the man's leg with the aforementioned tablecloth.

In a bizarre twist of events, the man sat smiling, even laughing. She looked up to him, down to his scalded leg. Up again. Down again. Then it dawned on her, and she knocked on his leg to confirm that it was, in fact, a wooden leg.

> Anonymous, server of nameless years, shared an embarrassing story. Oh, all right, I confess. The story I'm about to tell happened to me. I was serving a group of sixty people: an Italian family reunion. Upon approaching an older gentleman (probably the patriarch of the family), I was thinking, *Can I warm up your coffee?* and/or *May I top up your coffee?* Somewhere between my brain and my lips, the wires got crossed, and I asked, "Can I wop up your coffee?"
>
> An ominous silence flooded the room while I did my best Porky Pig impression, "Budu, budu, budu..." Thankfully, the Pincero family had a sense of humor, as they all howled with laughter. And th-th-that's all folks.

The final word on these matters may not be worthy of Confucius or E. F. Hutton; nevertheless, the survey recommends you shake it off, and try not to let it ruin your day. Just be as responsible as you can, and don't sweat the small stuff.

> Charles, server of twelve years and a self-proclaimed show-off, was preparing cherries jubilee for a table of local politicians and their wives. Charles had bragged on more than one occasion that no one can do flambé as memorably as he can.
>
> Well, when he added too much brandy then set it afire, the flame was more than he'd anticipated. With singed hair and eyebrows, his performance was undoubtedly memorable.

SERVER'S NOTES

Chapter 21

Responsible Alcohol Service

Although this book puts a great deal of focus on servers selling and up-selling alcohol, there are limits. Limits of propriety. Limits of common sense. Limits of customer safety. Limits pertaining to the law.

Did you know that if a customer gets drunk in your establishment and has an accident, a fight, or any other trouble, you and the establishment may be held liable?

As the laws are constantly in a state of evolution, this book will advise you, the server, to stay abreast of the laws in your area. And also advise you to keep a manager informed of any and all volatile situations which involve overindulgence of alcohol.

Although civil liability laws, liquor regulations and penalties are ever-changing, make no mistake, depending on your establishment's policies, type of liquor license, and location, penalties can include liquor license suspensions, revoked licenses, fines, and some violations can result in prison terms.

Many provinces and states are instating (or have instated) mandatory licensing or certification of F.O.H. employees who serve alcohol. Such programs ensure that servers, bartenders, door staff, security, managers, host staff, etc. are aware and able to handle a multitude of situations where alcohol is concerned. The surveyed servers unanimously agreed that we should all take any such courses that are available to us.

Issues like serving minors, serving after hours, serving intoxicated patrons, allowing patrons to drive while under the influence, etc. must not be taken lightly. In order to protect yourself from legal actions, you must first know a few things about the factors which affect how much an individual can drink before becoming impaired, how to tell if a customer is becoming impaired, how to help customers drink safely, and how to check IDs.

No two people respond identically to the affects that alcohol has on their faculties.

Factors affecting how much an individual can drink before becoming impaired are:

- Height
- Weight
- Fitness
- Age
- Medication
- Food consumed

- Body type
- Health
- Mood
- Gender
- Tolerance
- Environment

- Time between drinks

Despite the undeniable fact that individuals react differently to alcohol, a basic knowledge of common responses to alcohol can help us identify potential problems before they arise.

Some common signs of intoxication are:

- Loss of self-control and inhibitions
- Loss of judgment
- Loss of reason and caution

- Loss of intelligence and memory
- Loss of co-ordination and balance
- Impaired senses
- Problems with speech
- Physical changes
- Change in vital signs

Is a customer becoming loud, boisterous, red in the face or glassy eyed? Are they spilling drinks, losing their train of thought, slurring their words or breathing irregularly? If so, you must be prepared to handle the situation.

Ways to assist customers to drink safely are to:

➤ Be aware that a customer may have been drinking before he/she arrived.

➤ Watch for signs of intoxication.

➤ Keep track of the number of drinks being served to each person.

➤ Slow down service to help your customers pace their rate of consumption. Don't go past the table as frequently.

➤ Offer a non-alcoholic drink as a "spacer". Try bringing water or a free coffee.

➤ Let your fellow servers/bartenders know that you are trying to prevent your customer from becoming too impaired so that no one inadvertently serves the customer in question.

➤ Don't encourage an impaired customer to order when they still have a half-full drink. Wait for them to reorder.

➤ Serve food before, during and/or after serving drinks. A carbohydrates like bread works as an excellent sponge for absorbing alcohol.

What about underage drinkers? Simple, right? Just check their ID.

Not so simple. Identification can be altered, borrowed, counterfeited, even stolen. So, how can you tell if it's legal? When checking someone's ID, don't just glance at it, check it closely.

➤ Take it out of its case.
➤ Hold it. Does it feel right? Is it the right weight, texture, size, shape?
➤ Does it look right? Is it the right color? Is the photo faded in a way that may suggest color photocopying?
➤ Really look at the photo. Are the person in the picture and the person in front of you the same person? You'd be amazed how nervy kids are when it comes to borrowing a friend's ID.

Jerold, bar server of two years, checked a young woman's ID. With the dim lighting in the bar, he struggled to see that the numbers looked all right. However, upon closer investigation, he realized that the bearer, who was laying low under a baseball cap, was Asian. The person in the photograph was clearly African American.

- Check the physical description on the ID.
- Confirm information with the person presenting the ID. Do they know the address? Spelling of name? Date of birth? If you know your zodiac signs, a fun one is to ask them their astrological sign.
- Run your fingernail over the birth date. Has anything been taped on?
- Compare the numbers in the date of birth and the date of issue. Do they look the same? Are any of the numbers thicker? Darker?
- Is the date of birth clear? Look for smudges. Have there been any additions or omissions around the birth date?
- The expiry date and the birth date should match for the month and day.
- In some areas (check to see if your area applies) birth dates appear within a series of other numbers.
- Check for cut and paste numerals.
- Check for faulty lamination. Wrinkles or air bubbles may be a clue that the ID has been peeled open to make changes.
- Does the bearer look nervous?
- Ask for a second form of ID.

Now, provided customers are sober enough and IDs are valid, there are still other factors governing the sales and distribution of alcohol.

Since state/provincial laws and house policies are so varied, some question you may wish to ask your boss or local liquor control council are:

- What are the age restrictions on alcohol sales or service in your area?

- What forms of identification are acceptable?
- What, if any, is the Designated Driver program or policy?
- What is the maximum amount of alcohol per drink allowed in your area?
- What is the maximum amount of alcohol per person allowed in your area?
- If children are accompanied by parents and they wish to give their child some wine or beer at their discretion, is it legal?
- Is it legal, in your area, for an intoxicated person to remain on the premises?

There is one question regardless of location that you needn't ask.

The question: Is it ever legal to serve an intoxicated person?

The answer: NO! It is never legal to serve an intoxicated person.

In closing, be careful how you handle issues that are punishable by law. They say, if you play with fire you get burned. Just think how burned you'd get if you added alcohol to the fire.

PART FIVE

CHECK, PLEASE

In This Part

Chapter 22: Turn 'em and Burn 'em

Chapter 23: Check, Please

Chapter 24: Finishing the Job

Chapter 25: Bartenders, Bar Servers, Cocktail Servers, Drink Slingers, etc.

Chapter 26: Tips

Glossary

SERVER'S NOTES

Chapter 22

Turn 'em and Burn 'em

This chapter is not about turning the fryer upside down and lighting a match to the kitchen (although some days that may not sound like a bad idea). This chapter is not about rushing paying customers, either. It is about turning tables, which means:

Your section is full. There are customers lined up at the door. And you want some of those waiting customers to sit in your section so that you can make more tips. What do you do to turn your tables faster?

- Offer (as a favor to them) to order their appetizers while they look over the entrée menu.
- Inform them of the specials. Kitchens can usually (hopefully) have specials prepared faster than other entrées.
- Recommend other entrees that can be prepared quickly. You'll know which items can be prepared faster if you know your stuff.
- Suggesting desserts that don't need a lot of preparation (i.e. pie instead of a triple layer hot fudge sundae).
- Some establishments may even ask that you don't sell desserts on busier nights, opting for volume over the extra couple of bucks a dessert can bring to an average check.

Although this chapter may sound contradictory, after all the talk about sales and up-selling, there are times when you should forego a small sale for a larger sale or profit. Let's say a four-top orders two desserts, and let's say that those two desserts total approximately ten dollars. Now, think of the four people waiting in the lobby, losing patience, preparing to go elsewhere for dinner. The few minutes it takes to make ten dollars from the table sharing desserts could be used to sell rounds of cocktails and appetizers to the four people that get sat in your section because you were smart enough to turn and burn their predecessors.

> Conversely, if there's no one waiting to be seated and the tables aren't reserved, stick to your suggestive sales techniques and utilize every sales opportunity.

- Adhering to good table maintenance will remind the customers that the meal is over. People are less likely to hang around once the dinner table is cleared.
- Not waiting for them to ask for the bill. Make sure they have everything they need, ask them if you can get them anything else, them bill 'em with delivery of the last sale.
- Paying attention to billed tables. Swipe credit cards or make change as soon as possible.
- Staying on top of things. Get them anything and everything they need as quickly as possible, and they'll soon be saying, "Check, please."

Chapter 23

Check, Please

At last, time to collect on all of your hard work. But your work isn't done yet. There are still numerous things to keep in mind. You haven't got your tip yet, so keep your eye on the prize.

- Before you deliver a bill, double-check to ensure that everything is correct. Confirm that everything has been rung in or added properly.
- Inform customers where and to whom they should pay bills.
- Return with change or credit cards ASAP.
- Don't assume the change is your tip. If in doubt, return with the change.

FYI → When collecting a payment, NEVER ask, "Do you need change?" or "Would you like change?" It makes the customer feel uncomfortable or obligated. Instead, simply say, "I'll be right back." If they want you to keep the change, they can tell you at that point.

- Who gets the bill? Don't assume that the male is paying. An outdated sexist attitude can blow a tip.
- Thank them, by name if you know it.
- For larger tippers, it's a good idea to thank them twice. The double thank you shows appreciation, and returning customers will know that their generosity wasn't wasted or unnoticed.
- If they've requested separate bills, do not wait until the last minute to prepare the bills. Don't waste their time or yours.

About separate checks -- don't panic or expect the worst. Separate checks need not be a nightmare, provided you stay focused and take charge of the service. Most servers number seats or customers to stay organized. This sounds logical, until people start to mingle or switch seats.

A nice personal touch is to use their names to keep track. Customers should not be expected to remember their number, but they'll surely remember their own name.

FYI → For those who believe separate checks are all work and no reward, remember the previously mentioned statistics. 74% of the surveyed servers agree that people tip more on separate checks. Think about it…leaving a minimal percentage on a small bill may seem cheap, where one large bill can cause the aforementioned "sticker shock". A reasonable percentage on a higher bill may seem unreasonably high. Pooling money gives the opportunity to (anonymously) chip in a little less. But when an individual pays a bill, the server knows who tipped well and who scrimped.

This topic warranted reiteration because if your customers want separate checks, and don't get them, they could be thinking a million things. "That cheap SOB, Tom, always puts in less than his share. This time I'll let him pay extra." What if the SOB doesn't put in extra? It won't come off the bill. It'll come off your tip.

"Marcie drinks way more than I do. Why should I pay for her forth drink?" If Marcie, the lush, only pays an equal share, and everyone else pays less to account for her over-indulgence, again, your tip suffers.

"I paid more last time. Let someone else cover it this time." What if someone else doesn't cover it? Get the idea?

So...

You've topped the bill with mints and/or toothpicks and placed it on the table, all the while smiling. Phew, mission accomplished. Cool, this is the perfect opportunity to slip off for a smoke or a coffee, right?

Wrong!

If you disappear now, and the customer is ready to pay, you are gambling with your tip.

"The movie starts in ten minutes." "The babysitter charges time and a half after eight." Whatever. Bottom line is they want to leave, and you're nowhere to be found. If they're late for the opening credits, to whom do you think the blame will be attributed? Where do you think they'll get the extra money to pay the babysitter? The answers are 'you' and 'your tip'. Just because you've given them the bill does not mean it's over. You haven't been paid yet, so stick around. Don't hover, though. It's discomforting and rude. I know I just contradicted myself. Stick around. Don't hover. Stay close. Not too close. Contradictory? Yes. Correct nonetheless? Also yes.

Sarah, server of 12 years has advice for situations where customers are ignoring the obvious presence of a bill.

Whether the server is in a rush to get clocked out, or customers are not in a rush, sometimes customers seem to take an eternity to pay up. Sarah does, what she refers to as, the 'pop and peek'. This is when you pop by the table and peek at the bill, offering, "Can I take care of this for you?" When they confess they haven't even looked at the bill, she blushes. "Oops, sorry. No rush. I'll be back in a couple minutes, when you're ready."

Under these circumstances, most people fork up the cash to save you any further embarrassment.

Research shows between the hours of 2 p.m. and 5 p.m. many servers do side-work or take breaks, forgetting to check and see if their customers are ready to pay. Customers shouldn't have to hunt you down or ask every other employee in the dining room to swipe their credit card. Although you've given them dozens of reasons to leave a big tip, ignoring them at this point will overthrow all of your previous efforts.

After you've presented the bill and taken five to ten steps away from the table, turn casually to see if they're ready to settle up with you. If not, return to the table after a couple minutes to see if they're ready to pay.

Be alert when presenting the bill. Once customers have their bill, don't forget to finish the job.

Chapter 24

Finishing the Job

Before the billing stage of the dining experience, there are many other situations when servers may be inclined to do a mediocre job. Many of the following have been mentioned in other chapters. Now to consolidate and recap, let's start at first contact.

- Smile and acknowledge new arrivals as soon as possible.
- When greeting a table, be sure to introduce yourself.
- Explain any specials and assist with the menu if necessary.
- Sell and up-sell drinks.
- Sell and up-sell apps. Are you nodding?
- Get all details when taking orders, including preparation details, special orders, sides, etc.
- Be sure to offer extra sides.
- Maintain table maintenance throughout.
- Keep smiling.
- Offer drink refills throughout.
- Sell and up-sell wine.
- Pour and top up wine glasses.
- Be sure orders are delivered properly, with all the trimmings.
- Do quality checks in a timely manner.

- Sell and up-sell desserts.
- Sell and up-sell after-dinner drinks, coffees.
- Check the bill carefully before delivering it to the table.
- Stay alert! Take payment at the customer's convenience, not yours.
- Thank them, then keep an eye out to see if they have any other needs. Offer coffee and water refills just like you did before they paid. Your job doesn't end until they get up to leave and you say goodbye and thank them.
- Thanking all customers on their way out is mandatory. This practice does not have to be repetitious or sound mechanical. "Good night." "See you next time." "Goodbye, Mr. Brown." "Have a nice weekend." "Thank you." "It was my pleasure."
- Helping ladies with their chairs, helping any customer on with their coat or holding the door for them, can leave a lasting impression.
- Double check the area surrounding the table to ensure that nothing has been left behind (glasses, wallets, keys, etc.).

With all of the customers gone and your share of cleaning duties done, it's time to cash out, count your tips and call it a day.

In present-day establishments, cashiers are rarely seen, making servers responsible for carrying and keeping track of their payments.

Make no mistake, the aforementioned rules about customer service and finishing the job apply to all front of house employees (dining room servers, bartenders, bar servers, cocktail servers, drink slingers, etc.). All of us must give our customers the full treatment if we want to get a full tip

Chapter 25

Bartenders, Bar Servers, Cocktail Servers, Drink Slingers, etc.

You know who you are. If you've picked up this book and flipped immediately to this chapter to see if there is anything in here for you, the answer is yes! Since I have walked in all of your shoes and interviewed servers in every type of establishment, we can honestly say that the entire premise of *Service With A Smile* ☺ applies to you, as well. Some situations vary, but the long and the short of it is those who serve and those who tip.

> Paul, bartender/bar server of 5 years, has learned fast that people like to buy their bartender a drink; however, if he drank every drink that was bought for him, he would either be too intoxicated to work, or he would undoubtedly be fired when the boss caught him. Paul's solution to this dilemma was some creative economics. If someone bought him a shooter, he'd claim he was drinking tequila or Sambuca, covertly filling a shot glass with water. In the case of mixed drinks or cocktails, he'd simply leave out the alcohol and drink virgins instead. Rather than saying "No thanks" because of work ethic or policy and losing out on tips in the form of drinks, he converts the drinks into cash and spends the tips on his own time.

If you want to know where, specifically, to look for information pertaining to bar staff making better tips, you should go to page one and start reading.

The comments in Chapter 5, *Know Your Stuff* and Chapter 10, *Sell! Sell! Sell!* will offer a few specifics; however, reading the entire book from cover to cover is the best way for all of us to learn more ideas about how to improve your tips.

Chapter 26

Tips

Call them tips, call them gratuities, call them whatever you like, but know that these nickels dimes and dollars are what serving is all about: the Holy Grail for servers.

Let's face it; you're certainly not in the business for the slave wages or the simple gratification of a job well done. Granted, you may get a warm fuzzy feeling when you play a significant role in making someone's anniversary dinner or birthday party special, but admit it . . . tips. Tips are the bottom line.

You're probably wondering how anyone can use an expression like 'slave wages' and then continue writing as if nothing was intrinsically wrong with such a term. You're probably wondering how anyone can say 'slave wages' at all without being appalled or at least wincing. Well, I do so as a veteran server, who faced reality a long time ago. Reality is, servers make less per hour than anyone else in the free world. Less than everyone we work with, even less than the bussers, with whom most of us are expected to share our tips. That's reality. More reality…you can moan and groan yourself into a frenzy, or you can look at it the way veteran servers do. Every new table is a possible pay bonus. So why not utilize every angle to increase your tips?

The following are questions commonly asked by novice servers:

What percent is a good tip or even the norm?

Now that's a question! Our peers say, "Less than 10-15% sucks and more than 20% of the bill is awesome."

Many rookies ask how much they can expect to make in tips after they're trained. This question is usually directed to the trainer. "How much do you average in tips per night or per week?

There is a way to calculate this, without actually asking a peer to divulge confidential, financial information. This can be done as early as the interview stage provided a comfortable report exists between you and your interviewer. Ask what the average sales per server on any given night, or week, are. Be careful not to base any calculations on the establishment's busiest night of the week. Now, rest assured, even mediocre servers will take home ten to fifteen percent of their sales (depending on house tip-sharing policies). 100% of the interviewed servers agreed that any server who consistently takes home less than ten percent of their sales is in the wrong business.

Another good question is...Is it proper etiquette to tip on the total bill or the bill before taxes?

Although this question has been answered once, the surveyed servers asked for reiteration. Many consumers say, "Why should I tip on taxes?" Again, there are different schools of thought on this matter. What's proper?

Can anyone really say what's proper? This is one of those questions that must be left to the individual. However, there's nothing stopping me from rendering the servers' opinion.

The way we see it...many, even most, restaurants or servers have a policy about tipping or sharing tips with their support staff (*bussers*, bartenders, hostesses, etc.). The amount that is passed on or shared varies greatly, usually based on the servers' sales . . . including taxes. From the servers' standpoint...since we are tipping out on the taxes, why shouldn't the customers?

Income tax time. The mere mention makes you shudder, doesn't it?

How should you go about claiming tips?

Any practicing server would be asking for trouble if they were to spout controversial advice. So instead, let's say you're not sure exactly how much you made last year. In that case, you may want to ask several experienced co-workers (confidentially) how much they claim in tips each year. Logic would have it that servers working in the same place, with a similar amount of hours should make approximately the same amount of gratuities. The interviewed servers say that it usually adds up to about 10% of your annual income.

Without going off on a long moralistic or philosophical commentary about claiming tips, you may find it interesting that almost all servers (96%) claim the unwritten standard -- 10% of their income.

What's more interesting is that servers are expected to claim all tips at tax time, yet (in most if not all jurisdictions) tips don't count at pension time or in cases of unemployment or disability benefits.

All personal and interviewee opinions aside, you must know THE LAW: Tips are taxable income and must be reported to all applicable tax agencies.

Did you know: Al Capone was imprisoned on charges of tax evasion. Ironic, you can get away with murder, but you can't escape the tax man.

URGENT INFORMATION!

Failure to claim ALL tips can lead to:

- ➤ Prison sentences
- ➤ Additional tax
- ➤ Interest charges
- ➤ Check your local laws to find out more details for your personal situation.

WARNING!

Projecting a sense of entitlement when it comes to expectations of gratuities is unacceptable. Customers will not tolerate such attitude. Some of us forget that tips are not mandatory. In fact, tipping wasn't always as common as it is today. Generations ago, gratuities were only given for extremely outstanding service. It has developed into a customary practice over time. Sadly, the government got involved and, as a perk for restaurateurs, lowered the minimum wage for servers who receive tips.

Enough about that. Let's talk more about where your tips are found.

Who are the people who travel in and out your world every day? Call them customers. Call them guests. Call them diners. Call them clientele. Bottom line, they are potential tippers.

A piece of advice that veteran servers gave was "Don't judge a book..."

A common misconception of rookie servers is to give credit where credit isn't due. I'm referring to the potential of blue vs. white-collar tippers. Suit vs. steel-toed work boot tippers. Jack Fraser vs. Mark's Work Warehouse tippers.

What do you think? Do those who make more, tip more?

The survey says, "NO!"

Don't let a little dirt under the fingernails turn you off. Why? The logical reasons are as follows:

- Who is more like you, the man in the suit who sits behind a desk all day or the dude who built that desk?
- Who do your waitress friends usually date, the gentleman in the suit or the guy in the hard hat?
- Who appreciates manual labor more than manual laborers? Nobody.

> Rachael, server of fourteen years, says the largest tip she's ever received was from a large group of rough looking customers in Harley Davidson gear. Rachael says, of the retired bikers turned real estate investors, "Not only did they tip huge, but they were a lot of fun and ask for me every time they come back."

But wait! Don't misunderstand the point here. The point isn't to ignore white collars, but rather NOT to ignore blue collars. Be careful of karma. You are a laborer too and surely wouldn't like to be blown off at the dentist's office for someone in a white collar.

FYI ♀ Bonus for the ladies! Research shows that, overall, females make better tips.

In fact, studies indicate that women make nearly 5% more on average guest check.

FYI ♀ More good news for female servers. A simple touch on the hand, arm or shoulder when presenting the bill has been proven to increase a tip immeasurably.

WARNING!

The touch maneuver does not work for male servers. No matter how it's attempted, it invariably leaves customers feeling uneasy.

FYI → Another bonus for all servers. Some establishments set automatic gratuities (service charges) of 15% or 20% for special events, banquets, large groups in general. In this case, customers are typically notified during the booking process.

In closing, one last thought to ponder:

In the literal sense, you are feeding your customers.

Figuratively, their money is feeding you.

---

*NOTE - Many of the suggestions found in this book will depend greatly on the policies of your particular place of employment. Although this compilation of information is tried and true, you mustn't forget that servers don't make house policies, the bosses do. Therefore, it is recommended that you follow only the advice that is acceptable to your current employer.

GLOSSARY

This Glossary decodes common restaurant jargon used in *Service With A Smile* ☺. When a term is used in the book, refer back to this glossary.

This easy-find picture identifies merely a few money making tips, information and suggestions found within the book. For more, read thoroughly.

86ed a menu item that is temporarily unavailable

à la carte entrees that are served and priced separately

à la mode served with ice cream

al dente cooked firm to the bite (usually refers to pasta or vegetables)

apps. abbreviation for appetizers - dishes served before the main course

arm service a tem that refers to carrying dishes and beverages by hand, without a tray

ASAP abbreviation for as soon as possible

back of house staff (BOH) anyone who works in a kitchen: cooks, prep people, dishwashers, etc.

bar back a person who assists the bartender

bussers put in politically incorrect terms in the Oxford Dictionary as *"busboy(s) - a waiter's assistant who clears tables etc."*

chef also known as "head chef" or "lead chef" is the person in charge of all kitchen activities

deuce table of/for two

D & D (dine and dash) just like it sounds: eat and leave. The only problem is that some people do it without paying. That is what we call a D & D. D & Ds aren't something you come across every day, but they do happen. Sometimes, nice folks simply forget to pay and later return with cash and an apology. But other times D & Ds are well-plotted, premeditated scams. The scam artist will go to some lengths to throw you off, leaving a lit cigarette in the ashtray and slipping away, ordering a dessert or coffee and sneaking out, the old empty billfold left on the table routine, etc. I've even heard of a case where a guy left an old denim jacket draped over his chair.

dish-pig a term, meant in good fun, for dishwasher - a person who washes dishes

dish-pit dish washing machine and surrounding area

expediter a person stationed in the kitchen who is in charge of maintaining communication between the BOH and FOH.

float cash *esp.* small bills and coin carried by a server

four-top table of/for four

frappé served with finely crushed ice

front of house staff (FOH) anyone who works in the dining room: servers, hostesses, bartenders, bussers, etc.

FYI For Your Information

in the weeds too busy. If you're busy, you're busy. If you're too busy to provide proper service, you're in the weeds.

jargon restaurant speak. Words or expressions used by a particular group or profession, in this case, restaurant employees. Also: lingo, terminology, vernacular, dialect, etc.

line cook the people who work on the grill, fryer, stove and pantry are "on the line"; therefore, they are called line cooks. Line cooks are often referred to more specifically i.e. sauté cook, fry cook, grill cook.

neat straight up. Alcohol never comes in contact with anything, including ice.

pantry the area of the kitchen where cold items such as salads and desserts are prepared.

pantry cook the person in charge of preparing cold plates in the pantry.

pivot point a starting point or table location for taking food and drink orders, used for the purposes of organization and accuracy

premium liquors (rye/whiskey, rum, gin, vodka, tequila, brandy, scotch) available upon request. Premium brands typically have less impurities and, thus, are more expensive than well brands. Most establishment charge extra, some don't.

prep cook the people who prepare the food before it is cooked. They chop, slice, dice, defrost, ect.

rocks served on ice cubes.

rollups cutlery wrapped up in linen or paper napkins

section a group of tables for which one server or team of servers is responsible. Also called a station

service station where supplies for service staff are kept (water jugs, coffee pots and burners, cream, glasses, saucers, side plates, etc.). Also known as side station or side stand

spiel explanation of the restaurant, the menu, specials, etc., usually recited upon first contact

stiff(ed) when a customer pays the bill without leaving a tip

sous chef from the French "sous" meaning sauce. The number one backup person to the chef, the sous chef is second in command in the kitchen.

table tent a folded card advertising various foods, beverages or services offered.

tray stand / tray jack a stand used to hold service trays (usually portable)

twist unlike a wedge of fruit, a twist is merely a strip of the peel used as a garnish

underliner a plate that is served under a bowl, i.e., a saucer under a soup.

up spirits are chilled, then strained (often refers to martinis or manhattans)

virgin non-alcoholic (beverage)

weeded see "in the weeds"

well/house liquors (brands) the liquors (rye/whiskey, rum, gin, vodka, tequila, brandy, scotch) used unless another, typically more expensive, brand is requested.

PART SIX

APPENDIXES
Service With a Smile ☺

In This Part

A. *Top Ten Customer Pet Peeves Regarding Servers*
B. *Top Ten Server Pet Peeves Regarding Other Servers*
C. *Popular Red Wines Often Found in Restaurants and the Foods Which They Best Accompany*
D. *Popular White Wines Often Found in Restaurants and the Foods Which They Best Accompany*
E. *What About Hot, Spicy Food and Wine?*
F. *Why Drink Rosés?*

Appendix A

Top Ten Customer Pet Peeves Regarding Servers
(Based on the Opinions of 1000 customers)

I. Servers who don't smile.
II. Servers who ask, "Do you need change?" or "Would you like change?"
III. Slow, lazy service.
IV. Mixed up orders.
V. Indifferent servers who say things like "That's not my section."
VI. Uninformed/unknowledgeable servers.
VII. Insincerity. A fake smile is almost as bad as no smile.
VIII. Servers who moan and groan about their troubles. Tired. Sore feet. Etc.
IX. Rushing bills or service. i.e. Bringing food before wine. Delivering the bill without offering dessert.
X. Pushy sales tactics.

Appendix B

Top Ten Server Pet Peeves Regarding Other Servers
(According to 100 Surveyed Servers)

I. Servers who don't do their share of side-work, restocking, etc.
II. Table hogs/tip gluttons. Nobody likes a greedy co-worker who's always pouncing on the best tippers and trying to get the biggest tables.
III. Sloppy resets. Servers who leave their sections in a mess at the end of their shift make extra work for the next person who works that section.
IV. Those who don't follow basic courtesy rules like 'take a pot/make a pot', empty the mint bowl/fill the mint bowl.
V. Inferior assistance. When running dinners for another server, some don't finish the job (clearing, refills, steak sauce/condiments).
VI. Weeded servers who don't have enough sense to ask for help.
VII. Gossips.
VIII. Servers who won't help but have no trouble asking for help.
IX. No pride in the workplace. Concepts like neatness or pride in a job well done, cleaning up after oneself, poor table maintenance. Those who do a mediocre job make the restaurant (and everyone in it) look bad.
X. Servers who don't give the right of way to busier employees. These slackers are disliked for chitchatting and getting in the way of busy servers.

> Thomas, a server of 17 years, says, "If you want to brag that your middle name is Service, make sure no one wonders if your first name is Bad."

Appendix C

Popular Red Wines Often Found in Restaurants and the Foods Which They Best Accompany

Beaujolais
    Entrées: light meat dishes, ham, sausages, hamburger, pasta, pizza, grilled chicken
    Cheeses: light cream, Gouda
    Vegetables: tomatoes, beets, carrots, bell peppers
    Herbs/spices: ginger, mild chili, cinnamon, allspice, nutmeg

Cabernet Sauvignon
    Entrées: full-flavored red meats, steaks, roasts, lamb, duck, game birds
    Cheeses: mature hard and ripe soft, especially aged cheddar
    Vegetables: onions, shallots, carrots, green beans, bell peppers
    Herbs/spices: garlic, rosemary, thyme, dill, bay leaf, sage

Chianti
    Entrées: casseroles, spicy sausages, tomato-based meat dishes, pasta, pizza
    Cheeses: Parmesan
    Vegetables: tomatoes, mushrooms, truffles, bell peppers
    Herbs/spices: oregano, thyme, marjoram

Merlot
    Entrées: lamb, venison, game, turkey, meat casseroles
    Cheeses: hard cheeses
    Vegetables: eggplant, zucchini, squash, bell peppers
    Herbs/spices: oregano, thyme, rosemary

Pinot Noir
Entrées: grilled meats, game birds, veal, roast chicken, rabbit, salmon
Cheeses: soft
Vegetables: tomatoes, mushrooms, beetroot, truffles, bell peppers
Herbs/spices: basil, cilantro, chervil

Syrah/Shiraz
Entrées: highly spiced meat dishes, game, garlicky casseroles
Cheeses: mature, blue
Vegetables: ratatouille, bell peppers
Herbs/spices: garlic, black pepper, hot peppers, cilantro

Zinfandel
Entrées: rich meat dishes, venison, game, roast turkey, spicy pastas, spicy nachos
Cheeses: mature, blue
Vegetables: eggplant, bell peppers
Herbs/spices: garlic, pepper, fennel, cilantro

Basically, fuller-bodied wines go with fuller-bodied foods, and lighter-bodied wines go with lighter-bodied foods.

Appendix D

Popular White Wines Often Found in Restaurants and the Foods Which They Best Accompany

Chardonnay
    Entrées: fish, shellfish, deep-fried fish, poultry, rabbit, veal, pork, cream sauces, egg dishes, snails.
    Cheeses: mozzarella, Havarti, cream and other soft cheeses
    Vegetables: potatoes, carrots, onions, leeks, squash, celery, corn, mushroom, bell peppers
    Herbs/spices: basil, tarragon, chervil, marjoram, mace

Chablis (often referred to as a lighter, crisper Chardonnay)
    Entrées: fish, shellfish, especially oysters
    Cheeses: goat cheese, Munster, edam
    Vegetables: tomatoes, bell peppers, salads, including arugula and endive salads
    Herbs/spices: bay leaf, dill, lemon grass

Chenin Blanc
    Entrées: shellfish, sole, chicken, pork, light cream dishes, soy dishes
    Cheeses: Swiss, gruyere, Emmenthal
    Vegetables: corn, bell peppers, carrots, cauliflower
    Herbs/spices: basil, dill, mint, tarragon, caraway, nutmeg

Gewürztraminer
    Entrées: Oriental dishes, Thai, Japanese, light curries, smoked fish, foie gras (goose liver)
    Cheeses: Munster, limburger
    Vegetables: Spanish onion, asparagus, bell peppers
    Herbs/spices: ginger, mace, cinnamon, nutmeg

Pinot Grigio/Pinot Gris
 Entrées: seafood, salmon, duck a l'orange, venison
 Cheeses: Colby, Swiss
 Vegetables: green beans, potatoes, bell peppers
 Herbs/spices: caraway, basil

Riesling (dry)
 Entrées: fish, shellfish, game birds, pork, veal, Thai dishes, Chinese food
 Cheeses: Edam, Emmenthal
 Vegetables: tomatoes, bell peppers, salads
 Herbs/spices: cloves, basil, sage, lemon grass

Sauvignon Blanc
 Entrées: shellfish, fish, chicken, spicy sausage, prosciutto, vegetarian dishes
 Cheeses: goat, feta
 Vegetables: avocado, green beans, peas, asparagus, artichoke, bell peppers, fennel, salads
 Herbs/spices: oregano, thyme, chives, dill, basil, cilantro, capers, chilies

Basically, lighter-flavored foods go with lighter-flavored wines, and fuller-flavored foods go with fuller-flavored wines.

Appendix E

What About Hot, Spicy Food and Wine?

Highly spiced dishes can throw off the balance of many wines. If you want to match hot-tasting dishes, keep the following principles in mind:

- Choose wines with high acidity and some residual sugar (German Riesling, white Zinfandel, Vouvray, for example) rather than wines with perceptible oak flavors, evident tannin or high alcohol.
- For Mexican, Thai or light curry dishes select sweeter white wines, well chilled, such as Gewürztraminer or Riesling.
- Fruity reds with good acidity (Beaujolais and Valpolicella) when chilled will refresh the palate for mildly spiced dishes.
- For hot dishes that are also smoked, choose Zinfandel, Pecioto della Valpolicella or Chateauneuf-du-Pape.

Appendix F

Why Drink Rosés?

For some reason, drinking "pink" wine makes people "blush" with embarrassment. Why the bad rap? Beats me. But if you need justification to try rosé, here are sixteen valid reasons to enjoy a nice rosé:

  i. As a beginner program for non-imbibers.
 ii. In the backyard, around the pool, on a restaurant patio.
iii. On the hottest days of the year because it's the only wine you can serve on ice without looking like a Neanderthal.
 iv. When you're in a Goldilocks mood and other wines are too dry, coolers are too sweet, and rosé is just right.
  v. At breakfast or brunch with egg dishes.
 vi. At lunch with hotdogs, burgers, sandwiches, french fries, etc.
vii. As a compromise when you and your dining partner cannot agree on red or white.
viii. With a barbecue or a light picnic (in case you haven't gathered, it's a très chic outdoorsy treat).
 ix. To drive your snooty, wine know-it-all friend insane.
  x. Because sometimes red is too heavy.
 xi. With pork dishes, especially ham.
xii. To paint a romantic "dinner for two" picture.
xiii. To toast a pink sunset.
xiv. Because it's just too reasonably priced to resist.
 xv. Rather than drinking it with food, try it instead of food.
xvi. Just because you feel like it.

SERVER'S FINAL NOTES

Seminars With A Smile

To schedule a live guest appearance or hands on training program for your next in-house meeting, restaurant launching, mass hiring training session, convention, special event or trade show, e-mail for more information:

info@keynotebooks.com

A note from the author:

Since this book has taken nearly five dedicated years to research, compile, confirm, and publish, your opinions are important.
If you have *any* questions, comments, funny restaurant stories, or opinions please feel free to send e-mails to: christine@keynotebooks.com

Attention: Additional Copies

To order additional copies of *Service With A Smile* ☺ *Waiter / Waitress Training*, please contact the following: For speedy delivery and ultimate savings go to:
www.keynotebooks.com
or send inquiries to orders@keynotebooks.com

Or refer orders to:
www.thegreatamericanbookstore.com
www.bn.com
www.amazon.com
www.borders.com
Ingram Distribution
Baker & Taylor
Books in Print

Customized editions can be designed to meet specific needs i.e., addition of company logos and personalized introductions. Discounts available for quantity orders. For more information write to info@keynotebooks.com

KeyNote Books®

Printed in the United States
776000004B